John Ball of Hoylake

John Ball
of
Hoylake

Champion Golfer

John Behrend

Grant Books, Worcestershire
1989

The first edition limited to 1800 copies in cloth and
100 author's presentation copies

ISBN 0 907186 09 2

Typeset in Palatino 11/13
Printed by Severnside Printers Ltd.
Bound by Cedric Chivers

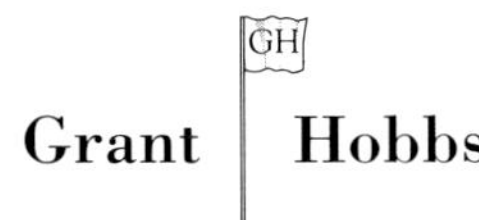

Grant Books
Victoria Square, Droitwich,
Worcestershire WR9 8DE

Contents

Acknowledgements		ix
Foreword by William C. Campbell		xi
Introduction		xv
Chapter 1	The Grand Professional Tournament (1872)	1
Chapter 2	Early Days (1875–1878)	5
Chapter 3	The Amateur Championship (1881–1885)	11
Chapter 4	The First Crown (1886–1888)	19
Chapter 5	Year of the Double (1890)	25
Chapter 6	The Title Defences (1891–1892)	33
Chapter 7	Success and Failure (1893–1895)	41
Chapter 8	Ball v Tait (1896–1899)	47
Chapter 9	The Boer War (1899–1901)	53
Chapter 10	Back on the Links (1901-1902)	59
Chapter 11	Victory on the Old Course (1903–1907)	65
Chapter 12	The Mascot (1908–1910)	71
Chapter 13	Westward Ho! (1912–1914)	77
Chapter 14	Post-War Years (1920–1940)	81
Chapter 15	In Perspective	87
Epilogue		93
Appendix		95
I	Ball's Open Championship Record	
II	Ball's Amateur Championship Record	
III	Club Scratch Medals	
IV	Prestwick Links in 1890	
V	Songs and Verse	

Acknowledgements

But for John Graham, this book would not have been written. When, as chairman of the Royal Liverpool Golf Club Museum Committee, he encouraged two or three of us to write a few pages about some of Hoylake's famous figures of the past, I drew the long straw, and started the necessary research on John Ball. Now, five years and many fascinating hours later, a book has emerged. Thanks go to John, for setting me on the road and for all the encouragement along the way.

Apart from the scrapbooks and minute books from the Royal Liverpool library, the main sources have been the writings of Horace Hutchinson, Harold Hilton, Guy Farrar, and of course Bernard Darwin; acknowledgement is due to A. P. Watt Ltd for giving me permission, on behalf of Ursula Mommens, Lady Darwin and Dr Paul Ashton to reproduce some of his splendid accounts of John Ball's triumphs. Extracts and illustrations have also been taken from a number of golf annuals and magazines—notably *Golf, The Golfing Annual, The Field, Golf Illustrated* and *Illustrated Sporting and Dramatic News.*

There are many people and clubs to thank. I hope all the Royal Liverpool officers and members who have helped in so many ways —with personal memories, with suggestions for research, and with advice—will forgive me for not mentioning them individually. From other clubs—thanks first to Bobby Burnet, the R & A archivist, for providing me with additional material, also to David Smailes at Prestwick, to Tony Nickson from Lytham, to John Goodban and Royal North Devon, Leo Leach of Leasowe and Oscar Lloyd from Holywell; also to John Pierpoint (sadly no longer with us) and Wallasey Golf Club.

Special mention must be made of Mrs G. Macdonald (Peg of Chapter 12), and of Lawrence Smith (John Ball's nephew) and his wife, of David Christie and of Leslie Edwards for a couple of his stories from the *Liverpool Echo;* thanks also to G. J. Aston for unravelling the mysteries of rail travel in the 1890s.

As for the illustrations, many have come from Michael Hobbs's golf collection, and others from photographs that he has taken specially for this book. I appreciate all his help. Thanks also should be given to PGA World Golf Hall of Fame at Pinehurst for the splendid photograph of Ball at the time of the 1924 Open, and, especially, for Peter Crabtree's assistance in making his library available so freely.

It is said that a writer's life has been made easier by the word processor. As far as I am concerned I prefer the animate, and so my grateful thanks go to Audrey Ellison for her patience and forbearance in typing and retyping from my distorted dictation and untidy scrawl.

Finally, Bill Campbell, as one would expect, has written a stimulating and generous foreword. I thank him sincerely for that.

Foreword

We all still need our heroes.

Our times seem to glorify money and worldly possessions, as though success can only be quantified. How refreshing it is, therefore, to read all about an amateur golfer whose outstanding competitive career extended for half a century, but who also charmed everyone by his unfailing modesty and consideration for others, and wasn't spoiled by his victories and fame. Just as his quiet virtues appealed to the golfing public then, reading about them is a welcome tonic in the current commercial environment. I am complimented and pleased to comment on this detailed yet lively tribute to the author's renowned and popular fellow member of the Royal Liverpool Golf Club in Hoylake, England.

As a visitor to this distinguished club for the 1953 Amateur Championship, I was intrigued by the large stairwell portraits of Bob Jones and the club's two amateur luminaries, John Ball and Harold Hilton. This positive impression has been verified and intensified by John Behrend's engrossing account of Ball—the man, the golfer, and the embodiment of the amateur spirit—of whom no less than Freddie Tait said, after losing a 37-hole Amateur final to his rival at Prestwick, 'I would rather be beaten by Johnny Ball than by any other man in the world.'

Ball was the first amateur to win the Open, in 1890 at Prestwick, where he had won the Amateur two years earlier; so again he beat the Scots both at their own game and on their own ground. He was thereafter a marked man in all golfdom, befitting the enthusiastic and prophetic support of his many friends in Hoylake.

The only remotely similar events in America are Francis Ouimet's epochal victory over Vardon and Ray in the 1913 US Open, which gave golf and amateurs a tremendous boost in the New World, just as Ball's Open victory at Prestwick had done in the Old World 23 years before; and, to a lesser extent Chick Evans' winning both the US Open and Amateur in 1916.

Ball's record in the Amateur Championship was remarkable, both in number of victories (8) and in their time span (24 years), extending from 1888 to 1912, i.e., from the age of 26 to 50. Of the nine Amateurs from 1887 to 1895, he won four and was runner-up once, and later won three of the six Amateurs from 1907 to 1912. Combining those two early and late periods, he won seven of the fifteen Amateurs and was twice runner-up; in the intervening period of nine Amateurs, he won only once, but he didn't compete in 1900 or 1901 because of the Boer War.

The only comparable Amateur record is that of Michael Bonallack, who emerged from strong fields to win five out of ten Amateurs from 1961 through 1970, the last three consecutively (which no one else has ever done). He beat three-time winner Joe Carr in the 1968 final and evergreen US Amateur stylist Bill Hyndman in 1969 and 1970, on this latter occasion by 8 and 7 after some phenomenal stuff at Newcastle, County Down. Michael was still only 35 years of age, so might have challenged Ball's record number of eight Amateurs, if his leadership had not been so successfully exploited, first as international team captain (resulting notably in the 1971 Walker Cup victory at St Andrews) and then as volunteer administrator in various positions of major responsibility in the game, culminating in the R & A secretaryship.

Bonallack did not have such a fluid swing, but he was strong and effective in getting on or near the greens, and thereafter predictably deadly. His holing out under pressure seemed to be as much by character and willpower as technique.

By contrast, John Ball was known for the beauty and reliability of his long game, thanks to a flowing and repeating swing with his driver and fairway cleek, but he was not a confident or reliable putter. So he and Bonallack, the dominant amateurs of different eras, achieved their great records by different combinations of special talents. Reserved yet motivated individuals, they both excelled as the competitive situation tightened in a match. They must have had strong nervous systems and stout hearts to go with their will-to-win.

Bonallack has not, to my knowledge, ever had the tendency which Ball shared with Bob Jones: an occasional early streak of poor play in major competition, as though they weren't fully engaged with the situation at hand. Time and again, Ball would get off to a poor start and then have to play his magnificent best to pull out the match. Perhaps, like Harvie Ward (the great American amateur of the 1950s), he was too relaxed a person to be on his competitive mettle unless and until he had to. Another factor may have been a holdover of his low personal confidence as a young man that had kept him from winning the Amateur until age 26, despite what he later said was his best golf in his teens. Here again we see a parallel with Bob Jones, who was a child prodigy, yet suffered the 'seven lean years' before breaking through in the 1923 U. S. Open at age 21.

John Behrend makes it clear that Ball was celebrated throughout the land, almost as much as he was revered by the proud members of Royal Liverpool, because of his abiding humility and amiability. Those innate and gentle qualities must have been considered, along with his great victories, by the eight clubs that accorded him honorary life memberships, including Royal Liverpool, the Royal and Ancient, the Honourable Company of Edinburgh Golfers, and Royal Lytham and St Anne's. Universal adulation of his virtues must have added much through the years to the 'ethos of amateurism' which has been so important to the game's traditions and so well represented by Bonallack, notably among other true sportsmen.

1990 will be the twentieth anniversary of Bonallack's last Amateur victory, the sixtieth anniversary of Bob Jones' improbable Grand Slam (including his only Amateur, which was won at St Andrews, the site of the 1990 Open) and, more to the point of this commentary, the centenary of John Ball's Open victory—the first by any amateur—and of his second Amateur victory as well.

So John Behrend's highly readable account of Ball's golfing genius and charm is timely indeed, and fortifies his place high among the game's truly great amateur players and heroes.

The reader is fortunate that this overdue tribute to John Ball—the golfer and the man—has been made by John Behrend, who holds his subject in such high esteem. The author's credentials include his own long-time fine golf game and being past captain of the Royal and Ancient and, more to the point, Royal Liverpool. He resides just off his beloved course's second fairway, and from his upper floor writing desk enjoys a commanding view.

John brings to this happy project deep knowledge of the game's history, as well as pride of place; and his book enlivens the club's rich heritage of amateur golf, which made it in 1921 the natural 'trial' venue for what would become the Walker Cup series. John Ball, Harold Hilton, Jack Graham and others had set the stage and the standards; and of the great amateurs in those exciting times in the growth of golf, none could rival the competitive record and good example and influence of John Ball, as so carefully researched and beautifully told here by John Behrend.

William C. Campbell
Huntington, West Virginia, USA
January 1989

Past President of the United States Golf Association;
Past Captain of the Royal and Ancient
Golf Club of St Andrews

Introduction

'Tell the editor that I can't think of anything that the readers would find interesting.' So said Johnny Ball when a reporter, helping with a new series on eminent golfers for a golf magazine, visited Hoylake to interview him shortly after his famous victory of 1890. Not only had he just won the Open Championship, but a few months earlier he had taken the Amateur title. No amateur had previously beaten all the professionals, and at the time harder to believe, an Englishman had for the first time taken the title of Champion Golfer from the Scots. It is difficult to imagine such a response from an Open Champion today, when the super sports stars are swept along by the tide of television. Why was he so reluctant to talk? Perhaps paternal advice was not to trust the press, or maybe it was just the natural instinct of a shy and reserved young man.

This was no isolated example. In an annual golfing review a couple of years later similar unwillingness was displayed: 'So reluctant is he to be led into any discussion as to his own merit as compared with those of any professional, that he will cheerfully announce his opinion that he would have no chance if a match was played.'

Nothing had changed a dozen years later when Henry Leach was compiling his book *Great Golfers in the Making*, in which the leading golfers of the time told their own story of their early golfing days, and how their game developed. Surely Johnny would have been one of the first to be asked to contribute, but there was no chapter about him. An article by Leach at that time revealed: 'We all know that he is an extremely modest man who is never interviewed, never writes articles, and never communicates facts about his personal history that he is able to hold undisclosed.'

None of this is helpful to a would-be biographer today. There was, however, one exception, for he did allow a few pictures of his swing to appear in Beldam's *Great Golfers—Their Methods at a Glance*, published in 1904, but the personal details were limited to his height, 5 feet 9 inches, his weight, 11 stone, and his year of birth, 1863, and the last of those was incorrect. There is some mystery about his age, for though his birthday was known to be on Christmas Eve, different sources have suggested each of the three years from 1861 to 1863. His birth certificate must of course be the final arbiter, and that confirms 24 December 1861.

Fortunately there is no shortage of the written word about how others saw him. He grew up in an age of class distinction, when professional golfers were deemed to be artisans. Those that purchased the newspapers and golfing magazines were more interested in the exploits of the amateurs, and there were more column inches written about them than about the professional game.

The Hoylake scrapbooks have made the task of researching much easier. They are attributed to Thomas Owen Potter, who was secretary of the Royal Liverpool Club from 1882 to 1894. Whether he started the burdensome task of cutting out and pasting in the weekly articles from *The Field* magazine, or whether he followed the example of a predecessor one does not know, but they contain the story of all the major golf competitions from 1869 for the next forty years. As the popularity of the game grew, and the golf magazines and articles proliferated, the annual haul of cuttings became more voluminous. One thin scrapbook would cover two or three of the early years, whilst later two thick ones would be required for each year. The thanks of all Royal Liverpool members are due to Thosper, as he was known, and then to Harold Janion, his successor, who carried on the good work. Above all, my personal thanks are due to them for these and the minute books and competition records of the club which have provided the basic ingredients for this story.

Golf has been well served by its writers, many of whom were players of distinction. Horace Hutchinson and Harold Hilton, both champions, and both of whom played many matches with Johnny, published several books, including accounts of these and other matches. H. S. C. Everard, John Low and Garden Smith could also write with first hand knowledge, but none has written more about Ball and with greater passion than has Bernard Darwin, and he helps, more than any of the others, to build a lifelike picture. If Johnny trusted anyone from the press it was Darwin. Occasionally he would confide some private fact or personal opinion—but would then add 'I ought not to tell you that because you write for the papers.'

I make no apology for the fact that what follows contains a liberal sprinkling of the writing of others. The language of the time hopefully helps to give the taste of the turf, and who am I to compete with masters of their art.

1 — The Grand Professional Tournament (1872)

The Grand Professional Tournament organised by the Royal Liverpool Golf Club in conjunction with their Spring Meeting of April 1872 seems to be a suitable starting point.

First let's set the scene. John Ball tertius, or Johnny as he was known, was aged ten at the time. He was the eldest son of John Ball junior, who had been proprietor of the Royal Hotel for about fifteen years. His father, Johnny's grandfather, had also been an innkeeper at the Green Lodge, so the 1851 census for Little Meolse, the southern area of Hoylake, tells us. By the time of the next census, ten years later, he was farming 55 acres of Lord Stanley's land with three employees. John Ball junior, as well as being landlord at The Royal, was tenant for the land surrounding the hotel, also owned by Lord Stanley. To the left was the racecourse, to the right high dunes, and ahead 'an extensive range of level grassland' which was cropped by sheep and infested by a multitude of rabbits. This was known as The Warren.

Three or four years earlier some Liverpool gentlemen had driven up the sandy lane, now Stanley Road, to the hotel in a waggonette and asked the landlord's permission to use The Warren for 'The Royal and Ancient game'. Once he had established what the game was, permission was granted. It seems likely that two of these gentlemen were James Muir Dowie and Robert Chambers. The former lived in West Kirby and had married the daughter of Robert Chambers of Edinburgh, one of the best known amateur golfers of the time. Doubtless they had first tried the ground in the West Kirby area and found it unsuitable.

So in 1869 the Liverpool Golf Club was formed with its headquarters at the Royal Hotel. The course was laid out by George Morris and Robert Chambers. George was

The Royal green and Royal Hotel in about 1870 from a painting by F. P. Hopkins

the brother of Old Tom and Robert Chambers was his patron, a relationship which meant that George travelled with him as his personal professional. Nine holes were sited, 'The holes being placed in positions to call out science in avoiding ponds and awkward banks', and the total length was just over 1 ˇ miles. George's son Jack was introduced to the club and appointed professional, though his main role was as clubmaker and greenkeeper.

Soon there were more than a hundred members. Many were from the wealthy Liverpool business community and had not previously played the game; others were from Scotland and from Westward Ho! The club had ambitions and the combination of Liverpool wealth and the Scottish connections through the Morris family encouraged the committee to invite the leading professionals. It was minuted in September of 1870:

> *The treasurer proposed to raise by subscription funds to the extent of £10 or £12 and invite one or two professionals offering them £2 to pay their expenses and prizes to the extent of at least £5 to play for. After discussions it was resolved to invite Allan of the Royal North Devon, Kirk of Blackheath and one or two Scottish professionals.*

The invitations were not, however, accepted though Tommy Dunn and young Tom Morris came on different occasions and played some challenge foursomes matches with members of the club.

Two factors encouraged a further attempt early in 1872. First young Tom had won the Belt outright with his third consecutive Championship victory at Prestwick in 1870, and in the following year no Championship was held. Furthermore the links at Hoylake had now been extended to 18 holes measuring just over 5,000 yards—a true test for champion golfers. So the time was ripe to extend a further invitation 'to all the leading professionals in Scotland and the few residing south of the border ... to the first meeting of its kind to be held outside Scotland'. This time the huge sum of £103 15 shillings was raised from members by voluntary subscription for prizes and expenses. The prizes were to be £55 and even allowing for the cost of the silver medal this left more than £40 to be divided as expenses amongst those that came. To put this into perspective, the total prizes at Prestwick when the Championship was restarted later that year amounted to just £20 with £8 to the winner. It was no surprise therefore that sixteen of the top professionals gathered for the tournament which was held on 25 April, the day following the club's Spring Meeting.

Despite the fresh winds and showers, weather not unknown at a Hoylake Spring Meeting, there were more than a hundred spectators gathered to see the champion tee off and one can assume young Johnny was among them. Tom made a poor start. He found a ditch at the second hole and took 8 at the 3rd on his way to 48 strokes for the first nine holes. Others fared worse at the start, Bob Kirk taking 17 shots at the first hole, and Tom Dunn 'twice hitting the rails which intersect a portion of the green'. Young Tom, despite it being 'not his day oot for stealing long putts' completed the first round in 85 (37 for the homeward half) and with a steady second round of eighty-two he overtook Davie Strath who had led by three shots at the halfway stage. So Tom Morris junior won the silver medal and £15. The full scores were as follows:

	1st round	*2nd round*	*Total*	*Prizes*
Tom Morris junior	85	82	167	£15
Davie Strath	82	86	168	£10
Bob Andrews	85	86	171	£8
John Allan	86	86	172	£6 10
James Anderson	88	84	172	£6 10
Tom Dunn	86	88	174	£5
Davie Park	92	84	176	£4
Tom Morris senior	92	84	176	(after play-off)
Bob Kirk	97	83	180	
Willie Park	90	91	184	
Dr Argyll Robertson	94	90	184	
Jack Morris	97	87	184	
Tom Hood	93	94	187	
Willie Thomson	96	93	189	
Mr John Dun	99	95	194	
Willie Dunn	100	94	194	
Bob Dow	113	96	209	
Mr David Brown	109	103	212	

There was more golf to watch and more money to be made by the professionals on the following two days. Scotland in the shape of young Tom and Bob Ferguson beat Bob Kirk and John Allan of England and pocketed a further £5 between them. Meanwhile Tom Morris senior took the first prize of £3 in a consolation competition for the unsuccessful professionals.

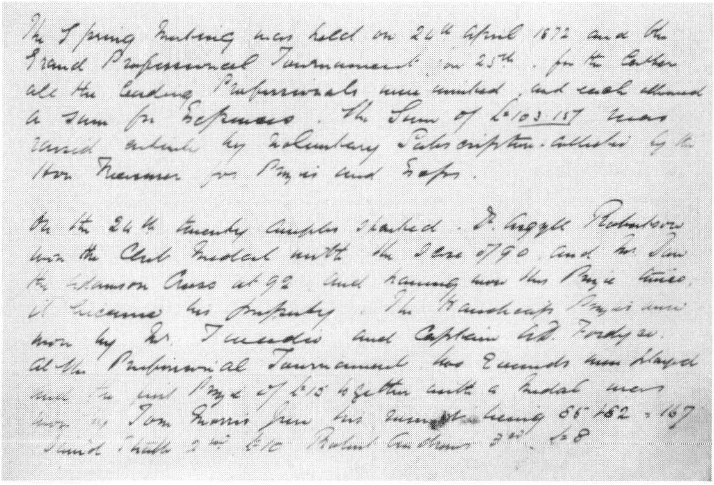
The Spring Meeting was held on 24th April 1872 and the Grand Professional Tournament on 25th. for the latter all the leading Professionals were invited, and each allowed a sum for Expenses. The Sum of £103.15.7 was raised entirely by Voluntary Subscription collected by the Hon Treasurer for Prizes and Expenses.

On the 24th twenty couples started. Dr Argyll Robertson won the Club Medal with the score of 90, and he [illegible] the [illegible] Cross at 92 and having won this Prize thrice it became his property. The Handicap Prizes were won by Mr Tweedie and Captain A.B. Fordyce. At the Professional Tournament two Rounds were played and the first Prize of £15 together with a Medal was won by Tom Morris Jun his [illegible] being 85 82 = 167 David Strath 2nd £10 Robert Andrews 3rd £8

Extract from the Royal Liverpool minutes for May 1872

Young boys learn from copying others and doubtless it was so with the development of Johnny's golf swing, for we are told that he was self taught with no lessons from Jack Morris. He will at any rate have learnt more from following the professionals on these three days than by watching his father. For though a useful player he was no stylist. He was new to the game when the club started, and in the first competition in the autumn of 1869 won the handicap prize with a score of 135 less 36=99. Eighteen months later he was scratch—rather more severe treatment than is meted out by the handicap committees of today.

The Boys' Medal

A few months after the excitement of the Spring Meeting, Johnny won his first competition, the medal for sons of members. Thus he became the proud possessor of Hoylake's Boys' Medal which is still played for today by those aged 15 and under. There is nothing so sweet as a first victory, and this and the inspiration of that professional tournament will have been the seeds of his prowess.

2 — Early Days (1875–1878)

The Royal Hotel, built in 1792 by Sir John Stanley to provide a healthy and invigorating holiday place for the gentry of Cheshire, was the only sign of affluence in Hoylake in the 1850s. The days of the great ships in the Lake had passed, due to the silting of the river, and it had declined to a village with a few fishermen's cottages. The building of the railway in 1866 began to change all that—though it was not financially viable at first and was closed, to be reopened in 1873. In the words of the *Morris Directory* for 1874: 'With its charming views of the Welsh hills,

284 HOYLAKE, CHELFORD, AND NORTHWICH ADVTS.

JOHN BALL,
"ROYAL" HOTEL
AND POSTING HOUSE,
HOYLAKE.

EVERY ACCOMMODATION FOR FAMILIES

This Hotel is pleasantly situated, adjoining the Seashore and the Racecourse, and commands a good view of the surrounding neighbourhood.

Visitors can obtain the right of SHOOTING over an extensive Warren of the Proprietor.

GOOD STABLING & LOCK-UP COACH-HOUSES.

Royal Liverpool GOLF CLUB held at the above Hotel.

From the *Morris Directory*, 1874

its sands admirably adapted for sea bathing, it may be safely reckoned, at no distant date, to become one of the chief outlets for the surrounding populace.' At the time there were fewer than a dozen houses between the Green Lodge and the Royal Hotel, and none to the west of the hotel. There was a further cluster of houses and cottages around Kings Gap and that was Little Meolse. Acres of sand dunes provided a barrier between there and Hoose, the district around Holy Trinity Church. But Morris was right. With the new railway, the prosperous Liverpool merchants built their great homes there, and the population grew from just over 1,000 in 1871 to nearly 4,000 ten years later.

From *The Field* articles a picture of the club and its golfing activities in the 1870s emerges. The magazine for 29 June 1872 tells us:

> *The summer season is in full cry and mightily keen foursomes and exciting singles are played by those who have been hard at work all day in the busy haunts of commerce ... here may be seen the most popular of steamship owners intent on driving the ball beyond the reach of the human eye as he was eager in the earlier part of the day to fix a steamer from an eastern rice port at £4 15 shillings ... here also is one of our most promising colts devoting all his energies to the requirements of the game, and as eager in pursuit of it as he was wont to be with the lasso on the plains of La Plata. Here too his coach in the game and companion in flowing beard, who also plays steadily and never loses his temper.*

The article continues with mention of a gallant ex-naval lieutenant playing with mine host of the Royal Hotel, a cotton broker and another colt 'whose skill at golf bids fair soon to rival his excellence at croquet ... Golf brings to Hoylake many who, but for it, would go elsewhere and is the means of gathering together a pleasant happy social community, cosmopolitan in its character too. We know of no game or amusement that evokes such enthusiasm.'

Members at Hoylake about 1874

At about this time a matchbook was initiated at the club. The games to be played were recorded and bets were laid. The results of these matches were included in reports sent to *The Field*. From them one sees that young Tom and Bob Kirk were back again in the autumn of 1872, and young Tom again with Davie Strath and Tommy Dunn the following year. They and other professionals regularly figured in the matches played at the time of the Spring and Autumn Meetings.

After Johnny's success in the 1872 Boy's Medal three years elapsed before he won it again. His score of 98 for 17 holes in 1875 was just good enough. There was plenty of competition for him then with Herbert Tweedie (the secretary's son), Herbert Farrar and Arthur Cook all capable of similar scores. This year too his name began to appear in the matchbook, though not with any notable success at first. It was the following year that signs of what was to come were revealed. In September a match against John Dun was recorded. He received a third (6 strokes) and beat him 7 and 6, after which three further matches were played on level terms and Johnny won two of them and halved the other. This was no mean performance for a 14 year old as John Dun with a handicap of scratch was the holder of the Club Gold Medal. A few days later another match was recorded between John Ball tertius and Davie Strath against Arthur Molesworth and old Tom Morris, and soon after he was playing Molesworth of Westward Ho!, who was recognised as one of the leading amateur players, on level terms.

To quote again from *The Field:*

The Club which is very prosperous offers great inducements to visit their links and the liberality of individual members is unbounded. No example is spared in bringing the best professionals from distant links and everything is done to encourage the Royal and Ancient game. Young players on the Hoylake links have but more opportunity of learning the style and stance than beginners on any other English links.

In addition Johnny had two other advantages. With the links a few yards from his front door he had endless opportunity for practice, and from his father he learnt the qualities of determination and self control. As for the liberality of the members, this will have been displayed to visiting professionals in the bar parlour of the Royal Hotel, and during the conversation with mine host the idea will doubtless have emerged of Johnny playing in the Championship to be held at Prestwick in September 1878.

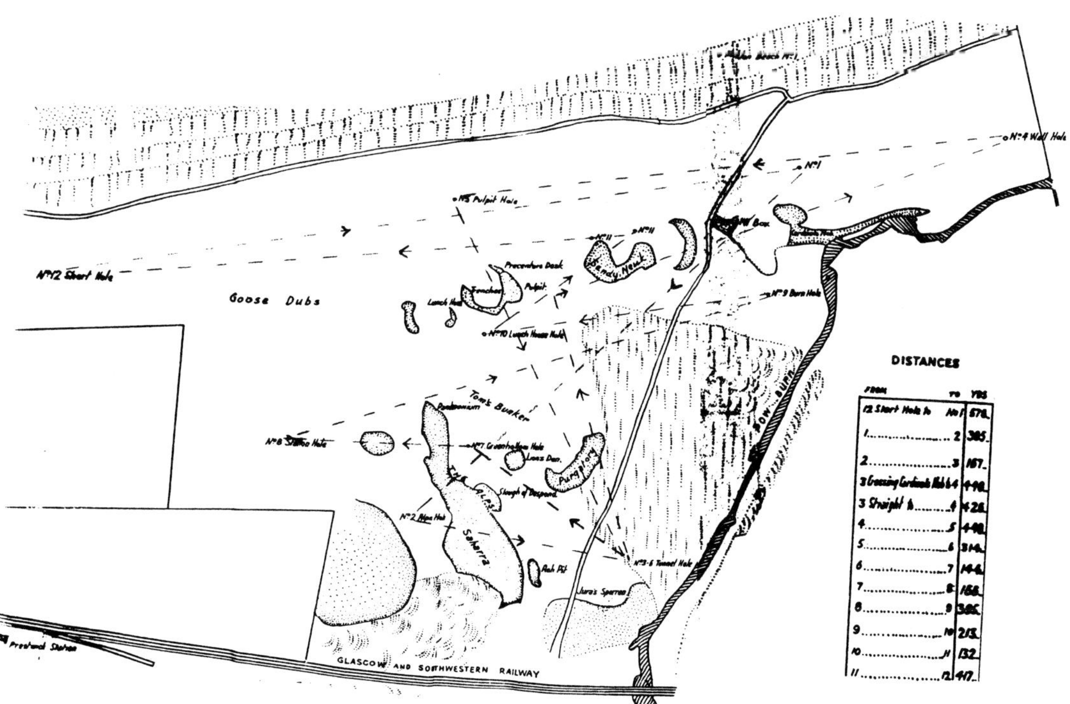

Prestwick in 1878

So Johnny headed north with Jack Morris and George Low to begin a championship career that was to cover 50 years. For a teenager, the journey itself will have been an adventure. To reach Liverpool Exchange station took more than an hour—via rail to Birkenhead Docks, horse tram to Woodside, and then ferry. Once at Exchange there was another eight hours' travel with changes at Preston, Carlisle and Kilmarnock.

Prestwick was one of three links used for the Championship since the trophy to replace the Belt, which young Tom had won outright, had been subscribed. It was a 12-hole layout measuring 3,800 yards with the holes criss-crossing, and in one case, following the example of another famous Scottish links to the east, the same green housing a red and white flag. Only the 2nd hole (the Alps) and the 5th (Sea Headrig) bear any resemblance to the Prestwick of today. In the field of 26 there were five past champions—old Tom Morris, Mungo Park, Willie Park, Bob Martin and Jamie Anderson, who had won the previous year at Musselburgh. Johnny was one of five amateurs playing and he was drawn near the end of the field with Bernard Sayers from North Berwick, 'the Wee Yin', just 21 years old and a mere 5 foot 3 who must have looked as young as his 16-year-old playing partner. He too was playing in the Championship for the first time.

After the first of the three rounds, J. O. F. Morris led with a 50 by three shots from five players, one of whom was Johnny. The others were Bob Kirk, Anderson, Park and old Tom. Johnny started his second round with an 8 and was not in contention for the Championship thereafter, although he made a good impression with the spectators; 'Mr Ball attracted considerable attention from the fact that it was his first appearance on a Scottish green ... he had also been playing well from the first and it was considered by those that knew the style of the Hoylake player that he had a good chance.'

J. O. F. Morris followed his opening 50 with disappointing rounds of 56 and 55 to complete in 161. *The Field* continues the story:

At the station hole Jamie (Anderson) had 17 to tie with J. O. F. Morris for the trophy, and as he said himself he could do it with 5, 4, 3, 5; the result showed that his calculations were not formed without some warrant. In driving off from the tee everyone thought he was in the pulpit, but on getting up to the ball it was found that he was distant about three feet. He made a tolerably good second shot and then off a full iron shot holed the burn in three—the greatest performance of the week. By judicious play he won the lunch-house hole in four. In playing to the short hole he was very much too strong and landed on the top of the hill beyond the hole. For a second his ball hesitated and then it slowly began to run back and finally dropped into the hole which hole was thus scored in one. The home hole was secured in a well played five, thus making his round 51 for a total for the three rounds of 157. It was now believed that the Championship was indisputably Anderson's, but Bob Kirk had still to be accounted with before the result could be declared.

One wonders how the sports reporter of today would have described Anderson's spectacular finish—two full shots holed. The language one suspects would have been somewhat more extravagant.

Bob Kirk was playing at the end of the field.

His third round was equal in steadiness to the other two (53 plus 55) and upon getting on the green at the last hole in three, it dawned upon the spectators that if he holed a long putt, he would tie with Anderson for the trophy. This information was conveyed to Bob, and, after a minute survey of everything between the ball and the disc, he made a magnificent attempt to put the ball within the circle. He was, however, a shade too strong, struck the iron lining of the hole, and rebounded out.

With no leader board to help the spectators it appears their calculations may have been at fault for Bob Kirk's final round of 51 left him two strokes adrift.

As for Johnny, his final round of 55 tied him for 4th place with Bob Martin of St Andrews, eight shots behind Jamie Anderson. A play-off for fourth place was held next day, but 'Ball thoroughly broke down' and Bob Martin's 55 was nine shots ahead. A money prize of £1 was the reward for Johnny's efforts, which on the advice of Jack Morris he put in his pocket, an action that a few years later was to give rise to some problems.

Jamie Anderson

3 — The Amateur Championship (1881–1885)

Golf historians might tell you that the first Amateur Championship was won by Allan Macfie in 1885. This, however, takes no account of the Grand National Tournament of 1858 held at St Andrews. The previous year a tournament to find the Champion Club had been initiated by Prestwick and the Royal and Ancient Clubs. For 1858 the committee decreed that it should be: 'a series of single matches to be decided by holes not by strokes and to be open to all gentlemen players who are members of any Golf Clubs'. This was to give rise to what was probably the first amateur status decision, for an entry was received from one Ronald Ross of the Bruntsfield Allied Club, Edinburgh, who was a very respectable young man but a venetian blind-maker, and therefore deemed to be an artisan. In the local St Andrews newspaper under the heading 'The case of the Rejected Golfer' the following report appeared:

There is an incident in connection with the arrangements of the tournament which has created some talk. We allude to the throwing out of one of the entered competitors. Amongst the entries for the competition was the name of one of the members of the Bruntsfield Allied Club who in accordance with the rules of the tournament paid his half guinea of entry money in May and the other half guinea before the balloting on Wednesday morning. Just before the time of starting, at half past eleven o'clock, he received a sealed note from the Secretary of the Union Club with his entry money of one guinea enclosed and also an extract from the Minute of a Tournament Committee Meeting held in the Clubhouse at half past ten o'clock of the same morning.

Apparently as an artisan he was not qualified under the third rule. Despite protestations that there were players in the field who are at least in no higher position in society than Mr Ross, the tournament went ahead without him.

One other unsatisfactory rule was 'in matches halved both parties be drawn again for the next set'. The ultimate winner, Robert Chambers, came in for some scathing remarks from the local press reporter on this account: 'Twice he drew a bye. He beat one man, a weak player, at the outset by four, and after that he had three halved matches in succession, and then won the deciding heat by a single hole' — and that single hole victory resulted from a three putt, the account of which should surely appear in any golfing anthology:

A low murmur of expectancy ran along the accompanying crowd, all-square and one to play ... both were close up to the green in three. Mr Chambers then laid the odds dead, leaving Mr Wallace the chance to win at the like from a distance of about four clubs' length. Alas, Balgrummo, ... thy right hand had lost it cunning on that fated green—that steady right hand which erstwhile had insinuated many a far away steal into the astonished hole. Mr Wallace looked from behind and from before, and then amidst breathless expectancy struck his ball. Short, short, Balgrummo short by at least a club's length, and not quite dead. Again Mr Wallace eyed his important stroke and—would we could write otherwise—missed. Mr Chambers had won the tournament by a stroke.

Robert Chambers could thus stake his claim as the first Amateur Champion.

Although a similar tournament was played the following year with both scratch and handicap classes it was not continued thereafter. Maybe the Prestwick thoughts had turned to the competition for a certain Belt.

Robert Chambers wins the Grand National Tournament in 1858

Some twenty years later the columns of *The Field* began to promote the idea of a national golf trophy for amateurs. Suggestions emerged that it should be played alternately at St Andrews, Hoylake and Westward Ho! and that it should be decided by strokes, two rounds of 36 holes; even the committee composition was proposed. Another proposal then came in letters signed by 'St George' and 'St Andrew' that an England versus Scotland match for amateur golfers should be held. The names of Ball, Hutchinson, and Molesworth were freely canvassed to represent the former, so Johnny's fast-growing skill was widely recognised. His game had continued to develop following his excursion to Prestwick for the Championship, but he was still too young to become a member of the Royal Liverpool Club. There were however the matches at Hoylake and holiday trips to Scotland. In August of 1881, following a visit to Machrihanish he arrived at North Berwick for a match between Royal Liverpool and Tantallon. He played against Mr A. MacKenzie Ross of the Burgess Club, one of the leading Scottish amateurs, with a large crowd following the game. His play that day was something special: 'Better and more dashing (as well as careful) play than this exhibited by the Hoylake representative in the latter portion of the final round we never saw, and it was no disgrace to succumb to it. Nothing was missed, he could not do wrong and the most difficult shots were done with the apparent unconscious ease.'

Soon he was making his mark as a Royal Liverpool member. In the club minute book for 3 October 1881 we read — 'The usual ballot was held when Messrs A.H. Cowie, John Ball (ter), W.B. Rook and D. Laybourn' — the secretary in his hurry forgot to add the words 'were duly elected'. No matter. The next entry was 5 October: 'The Autumn Meeting first day — Dowie Cup — won by Mr John Ball (ter) 84' And two days later: 'The Kennard Gold Medal won by Mr John Ball (ter) 87'. A month later he was winning the St Andrews Meeting, and off a handicap of plus 4 the Christmas Bank Holiday competition. Successes continued the following year with victories in four of Hoylake's six Scratch Medals, and his handicap by October had settled at plus 6.

The Tantallon Match

It was not surprising that the Hoylake locals were prepared to back Johnny against any Scottish amateur. This challenge was presented through the columns of *The Field* in the summer of 1883, where, shortly before, it had appeared, from no less an authority than the grand old man, Tom Morris, that 'Mr Ball is the best amateur player in the world.' The challenge was taken up on behalf of Douglas Rolland who had just played in the Championship at St Andrews and finished in 10th place, the leading amateur. He came from Earlsferry by Elie in Fife, and was renowned for his long hitting. The match was fixed for early December on a home and home basis, with the first 36 holes played at Elie, three rounds of 12 holes. There were to be no large money stakes beyond the expenses of the players, but there was considerable outside betting. Play started at 10 am with a large crowd including many from St Andrews. Rolland's home advantage and abysmal putting by Johnny on the first round left the latter trailing by seven holes. He lost two more in the second round. At least there was no wasted time, for after a good interval for lunch the third round started at 1.30, but by the end of the day Johnny had failed to make up any of the lost ground. Robert Chambers had umpired the match and in

Douglas Rolland

his speech at the conclusion remarked that 'the driving beat anything he had seen before', but there were no such compliments about the putting.

Johnny's confidence had been undermined and back at Hoylake rounds of 90 and 91, far below his normal form, meant that Rolland won the challenge, the bye, and the 36 holes at Hoylake. He remained for a further day for another 36 holes, despite or because 'he ought to have attended a summons in a local court in Scotland, due to an affair of gallantry'. Clearly he was a bit of a wild man, but wherever he went he was 'loved, admired, forgiven'. Anyway, next day Johnny was in command for most of the match, but from 4 up and 5 to play his game fell apart and Rolland won again.

So the Hoylake supporters lost their money, including young Harold Hilton, who wagered a shilling on his hero against a fellow pupil at his Norfolk school—no doubt a Scot.

This was all a great disappointment for Johnny and his supporters, but not quite as disastrous as the professional match a few years earlier when Jamie Allan from Westward Ho! accepted the challenge of Bob Kirk over four greens. Kirk lost by 28 holes with 27 to play and the match was over before he returned to his native St Andrews—the fourth venue.

This setback did not discourage Hoylake from its ambition to initiate a tournament to establish the Champion Amateur Golfer for the year. The memory of the defeat at the hands of Douglas Rolland had soon been purged by Johnny; for next May he inflicted a crushing defeat on Johnny Laidlay, another of Scotland's crack players, and a name that was to recur time and again in the years ahead.

Johnny Laidlay in play

In Thosper's own hand the following words appeared in the minutes of a council meeting on 13 December 1884.

Mr Potter then brought up the subject of a tournament to be played during the Spring Meeting open to all amateur golfers. He explained the project that had originated with him and read a good many letters which he had received. A discussion followed but it was agreed no decision could be come to, more especially as Mr Alex Brown and Mr T.R. Bulley had to leave before the close of the meeting.

At the next meeting all were agreed that a grand golf tournament should be played but there were two issues to be resolved. Firstly the extent of the club's financial support, and secondly whether it should be open to all amateurs, as Potter thought, or just those from invited clubs. In a passionate plea to the club general meeting that followed, the captain—James Cullen—emphasised that it was not in the best interest of golf for a valuable prize of, say, £100 to be won by a fisherman or a weaver from Scotland—shades of the venetian blind-maker's returned entry fee. Compromise won the day and the wording 'amateur golfer from recognised golf clubs' was agreed. Still some problems on the definition of an amateur remained. These were clarified in the following statement:

The Committee will naturally regard as not an amateur, anyone who makes clubs or balls for sale, carries clubs for hire, or takes fees from other players for playing with them or instructing them in the game; they will probably also exclude any player who has accepted a money prize in a competition open to allcomers; at the same time if it is many years since the player has done this there seems no reason why he should not by lapse of time be held to have regained his status as an amateur.

This was the edict of the committee appointed, and thus it was that John Ball, despite the pound he had won at Prestwick, was eligible, and Douglas Rolland, a money winner in the 1884 Open, was not.

Entries were coming in fast; the course, now extended to 5,400 yards was in good order, and there were high hopes of a home victory arising from Johnny's record score of 76 during the Easter Meeting.

Once the Championship had started it was evident that there was one other aspect that the committee had failed to solve satisfactorily—the draw. Forty-four competitors had arrived to play, and with the rule that both went through in a halved match it was not surprising that at the end of the second day three players remained, which is not a good number for contesting a semi-final or a final. Johnny had proceeded to that point by means of wins of 8 and 6, 7 and 6, 4 and 3 against his father, and 5 and 3 against Dr Argyll Robertson. The third day of the meeting was, however, given over to the stroke competition for the Club Gold Medal. Johnny's form was maintained and he won both scratch and handicap prize with a brilliant 77.

The following morning the Championship was resumed. He was to meet Horace Hutchinson, whilst Allan Macfie received a bye to the final. The morning match attracted a large crowd, and the day was fine with a stiff breeze from the south west. The story of the first nine holes was that Johnny's long game was in splendid order, but a missed putt by him, and two fine approach shots by his opponent to save the Cop and Dowie holes, meant that he was only one ahead at the turn. *The Field* reporter tells the story of the second nine:

On driving off from the tee homewards Mr Ball drove a clinker, Mr Hutchinson being carried by the wind into the field, thus making Mr Ball two up. Such however is golf that Mr Hutchinson went away with the next two holes in 4 and 3 against his adversary's 6 and 4 thus squaring matters. Mr Hutchinson took the next two holes in

4 and 3 against 5 and 4 this magnificent game making him two up, he having won the last four holes running. In playing the Field Mr Ball had a chance of winning the hole in 4 but missed a longish putt, the hole being halved in 5. Both competitors lay well on the course in their second for the Lake hole. Mr Ball played a magnificent cleek shot straight in the teeth of the wind laying himself almost dead. Mr Hutchinson in his third shot was twelve yards from the hole and showed what he was made of by holing his putt. Mr Ball not to be denied holed his also which elicited a ringing cheer from the crowd. Mr Hutchinson was now dormie two. On playing off for the Dun hole Mr Hutchinson played a long ball which got trapped in the ditch at the corner. Mr Ball wisely keeping clear and laid his second shot ten yards from the hole. Mr Hutchinson getting well out with his second lay within two yards of the hole in his third. Mr Ball taking great care over his putt was rewarded by gaining the hole in three. This made the game most exciting, Mr Hutchinson being 1 up and 1 to play. Both drove well from the tee, but Mr Hutchinson's second shot being stone dead from his iron proved too much for Mr Ball who was thus beaten by two holes.

Horace Hutchinson

Both were round in 80 and all were agreed that it was one of the finest matches ever played on the Hoylake links.

Reaction set in for Hutchinson in the afternoon. Macfie's steady 41 to the turn put him five up and the match ended on the 12th green. So Allan Macfie became Champion Amateur Golfer for the year—a worthy one, despite only halving his match in the first round, despite needing a hole in one at the Rushes to achieve his narrow victory over Mr W. de Zoete in the fourth round, and despite his bye to the final.

The remainder of the 1885 golfing season was, for Johnny, largely one of disappointments. In September the Dalhousie Club at Carnoustie promoted an even more ambitious golfing week than Hoylake's Spring Meeting. A similar matchplay event for amateurs, and strokeplay events for both amateurs and professionals with valuable prizes were arranged; as however it was an invitation event it did not rank as a true amateur championship. Johnny entered for this, and for the Open Championship that was to be held at St Andrews at the end of the following week (the earlier part of the week being reserved for the R & A Autumn Meeting). He lost at Carnoustie in the third round to a fellow Hoylake player F. Maitland Dougall to whom at Hoylake he would have conceded five strokes. It was John Laidlay who went on to win the matchplay event. So he moved on to St Andrews and the Open. From reports of his practice rounds it appears that his form remained inconsistent, and he failed to restore his game for the Championship. His performance was

Golf Tournament for the Amateur Championship
Open to all amateur members of recognised Golf Clubs
Held at Hoylake during the Spring meeting week
20th 21st and 23rd April 1885.
Entrance fees of £1.1/ each. and 25 guineas added by the club to constitute the Prize, a piece of plate (subject to the deduction of a second Prize value £10).

First Round.

Mr. J. Ball tertius beat. Col. E. H. Kennard 8 up and 6 to play
Mr. B. Hall Blyth beat. Mr. A. H. Doleman 3 up and 2 to play
Mr. H. S. C. Everard beat Mr. J. Sharp Junr. 2 up and 1 to play
Mr. J. Ball Junr. beat. Mr. G. A. Gilroy 4 up and 2 to play
Mr. Jas Duncan beat Mr. F. Muir 4 up and 3 to play
Mr. John Dun and Mr. Jas Wilkie halved

Third Round.

Mr. J. Ball tertius beat Mr. J. Ball Junr. 4 up and 2 to play
Dr. Argyll Robertson beat Mr. John Dun 6 up and 5 to play
Mr. Horace Hutchinson beat Mr. W. J. Mure 4 up and 3 to play
Mr. W. More Junr. beat Mr. F. H. Maitland-Dougall 2 up and 1 to play
Mr. A. F. Macfie beat Mr. Thos. Gilroy 2 up and 1 to play
Mr. W. M. de Zoete beat Mr. S. Mure Fergusson 8 up and 6 to play

Fourth Round.

Mr. J. Ball tertius beat Dr. Argyll Robertson 5 up and 3 to play
Mr. Horace Hutchinson beat Mr. W. More Junr. 5 up and 3 to play
Mr. A. F. Macfie beat Mr. W. M. de Zoete 2 up.

Fifth Round.

Mr. Horace Hutchinson beat Mr. J. Ball tertius 2 up
Mr. A. F. Macfie (a bye.

Sixth Round.

Mr. A. F. Macfie beat. Mr. Horace Hutchinson 7 up and 6 to play and won.

Extract from the Royal Liverpool minutes for May 1885

The first Amateur Championship — The Royal green

summarised by the simple words, 'Mr Ball did not give in his cards.' It is strange that 36 years later Bobby Jones, on his first visit to the Old Course, suffered the same fate.

4 — The First Crown (1886 - 1888)

Following the successful inauguration of the championship at Hoylake the previous May, a meeting was held in Edinburgh to discuss the next step. A trophy, value not exceeding £100, was to be purchased, subscribed by 24 principal clubs, and to be held in the custody of the club from which the winner entered. The two problems of the previous year were ironed out, with a clear definition of an amateur golfer, and a draw that, with all matches played to a finish, and with byes limited to the first round, would produce the correct number for the final. North Berwick had been picked as the venue, but as the dates were not suitable to the club, it was transferred to St Andrews to be held at the conclusion of their Autumn Meeting.

A small contingent from Royal Liverpool headed north with Johnny amongst them. Once again he progressed through the early rounds with something to spare. On the afternoon of the second day he met John Laidlay for a place in the semi-final, and followed by a large crowd he won at the 16th hole, though in the words of the match report 'the scoring was rather high'. Next morning he was confidently expected to beat Harry Lamb from Wimbledon, but 'Ball's play was wretched; his troubles seemed to be as many as Job's. He was entirely off both driving and putting and it seemed as if he had retired from the business.' It would appear from a detailed report of this match that his scores for the nine holes to the turn were 7, 7, 6, 5, 7, 5, 9, 4, 4 = 54. Not surprisingly the match ended at the 12th green. So, for the second time, the Old Course had exercised her capacity to humiliate.

John Ball — father and son

Next year the competition, now firmly established as the Amateur Championship, came back to Hoylake. Local hopes were high again. This time Ball father and son both reached the semi-final, Johnny to play J.G. Tait and his father against Horace Hutchinson. At the halfway stage the son was three down and father two up. The younger Ball played home without fault and won his match at the Dun. Meantime Ball senior held on to a lead and with only two to play a family final looked more than a possibility— a fact that was not overlooked by the father, who tempted providence by commenting accordingly to his opponent. This was an added spur to Hutchinson who duly won the last two holes. The final was a tense affair with many mistakes, culminating at the Lake (16th hole) when Johnny, one up at the time, heeled his tee shot into the field, and then playing another broke the shaft of his favourite brassie. Another missed drive at the last hole allowed Horace Hutchinson to complete his second successive victory in the Championship.

John Ball follows a tee shot

So the Hoylake members suffered this further disappointment. Did Johnny have the courage and character to win? When would his invincibility within the club be translated to the national scene—for he was invincible at Hoylake. The year of 1887 saw a club achievement that has not been matched since, and is never likely to be, for he won each of the six scratch medals at the club's principal meetings. His average score for those six rounds was a fraction over 80. Since he had joined the club in 1881, of the 39 scratch medals that had been competed for 28 had fallen to Johnny, and in that time, with a handicap ranging from plus 4 to plus 7, he had won 15 of the net prizes, and stocked the Royal Hotel with silver tankards, beer jugs, dessert spoons, salt cellars, biscuit dishes, salad bowls and goodness knows what else.

No one amongst the writers on golf at the time was better able to make a judgement on him than Horace Hutchinson. Although his book *Golf and Golfers* was not written until some ten years later, the section entitled 'The Portrait Gallery' throws light on both his character and his style. On his failure to win away from

The five scratch medals

The Dowie Cup

Hoylake he wrote 'possibly it was Mr Ball's modesty that prevented him from doing better abroad. It was a long while before he seemed to have a belief and a confidence in himself.' As for his style:

It is the present writer's opinion that Mr Ball's driving was the prettiest sight that golf had to give a man. I have never seen a player whose hitting was such a pleasure to watch, such a beautiful exhibition of grace and power, showing such ability to concentrate in a moment, and on a spot, all the muscular power that a human frame was master of. It was a beautiful sight.

Later in the article he commented on the effortless freedom with which he let his right shoulder come away, under and round. Indeed this impression may have been created by the one area of his style that was open to criticism, the grip—the club being held firmly in the palm of the right hand with the hand under the shaft and knuckles pointing to the target. This is the method he acquired by watching the Scottish professionals who had visited Hoylake in the early years.

Johnny's skill at this time was long driving and his play with the cleek. He had the ability to produce the shot required for the occasion.

He could cut a ball up out of a bad cuppy lie; we could all do that, all of us that are golfers at all, but Mr Ball was not content with that. He would cut the ball out and away it would go making for the right hand of the hole; but then it would suddenly catch sight of the putting green, or Mr Ball would begin to work on it after his manner, as if he had it like a Brennan torpedo at the end of a wire; it would begin to turn inwards towards the hole, announcing the astonishing fact that although he had cut it out of a hole, he was still able to put pull on it.

Johnny's grip

His more normal shot was the low flying ball which would rise towards the end of its flight and drop lifeless often beside the pin. Why then could he not win? Was it because 'he has played brilliantly all this while in the face of a constant besetting weakness—a tendency to miss short putts. Nervousness on the putting green has always been wasting away Mr Ball's extraordinary powers in the longer game.'

The venue for the 1888 Championship was Prestwick. Johnny went in a confident mood arising from a visit to Lytham St Anne's Club in April where he beat his record of the previous year with a brilliant 73, 'though he was rather heavily handicapped owing eleven strokes, thus only coming in third.' He will also have set off with good memories from his experience of ten years earlier, though the links had been changed and extended to eighteen holes, more recognisable as the Prestwick that we now know. 'The meteorological deities smiled auspiciously on the occasion', and with a bye and two easy victories he found himself in the fourth round. Here he faced James Mansfield from the Honourable Company and this turned out to be his closest match. Despite a splendid outward score of 36 he won only at the 17th. A 4 and 3 victory next morning matched him again with John Laidlay in the final. 'It not infrequently happens that when Greek joins Greek the tug of war is not characterised by any remarkable deeds of derring do, and such was the case here.' It was not Greek against Greek but Englishman versus Scotsman, and England quickly gained the advantage and kept up the pressure so that Scotland's game fell apart. Thus Johnny took his first Amateur Championship and returned to Hoylake with the coveted trophy and with the doubts as to whether he had the temperament for the big occasion finally allayed. The Prince of Hoylake had been crowned.

As for his prize, in addition to a Gold Medal he was permitted to choose an article to the value of £8. His choice was a double barrel shotgun—interesting as at the time the problem of rabbits on the links at Hoylake was becoming more serious. The minutes of the May council meeting tell us that:

> *Some discussion arose upon the best way of keeping down rabbits. Mr Graham proposed that we buy the exclusive rights of shooting the rabbits or otherwise keeping them down from Mr Ball for £20 per annum. This did not meet with unanimous approval and eventually the Captain and Mr Graham were empowered to make the best arrangement they could (not exceeding £20 per annum) with Mr Ball and, if he refused, then with Mr Tyrer.*

It appears that Mr Ball was a hard negotiator, and as at the same time the club were wanting to extend their clubroom at the Royal Hotel, the matter had to be handled carefully. In the end the captain and Mr Graham could do no better than £25, and that was on the understanding that Mr Ball and his son still had the right to shoot rabbits for their own use after the agreement was made. With Johnny's new gun one can be sure that rabbit pie will still have been on the menu at the Royal Hotel.

A watercolour by Thomas Hodges of John Ball Junior, painted 1889

5 — Year of the Double (1890)

The putting greens are such as are nowhere equalled. They are not flat, but so perfectly true that the effect of the undulations maybe calculated to a nicety. The fairly struck ball goes stealing along over them long after it seems as if it ought to stop ... One green, of course, differs from another in glory; but on the whole they are probably the best in the kingdom of golf.

This was Hoylake, the venue for the Amateur Championship of 1890 as described in an article of 7 June of that year in a series on famous links. The course then measured about 5,700 yards,but let the *Saturday Review* tell us more.

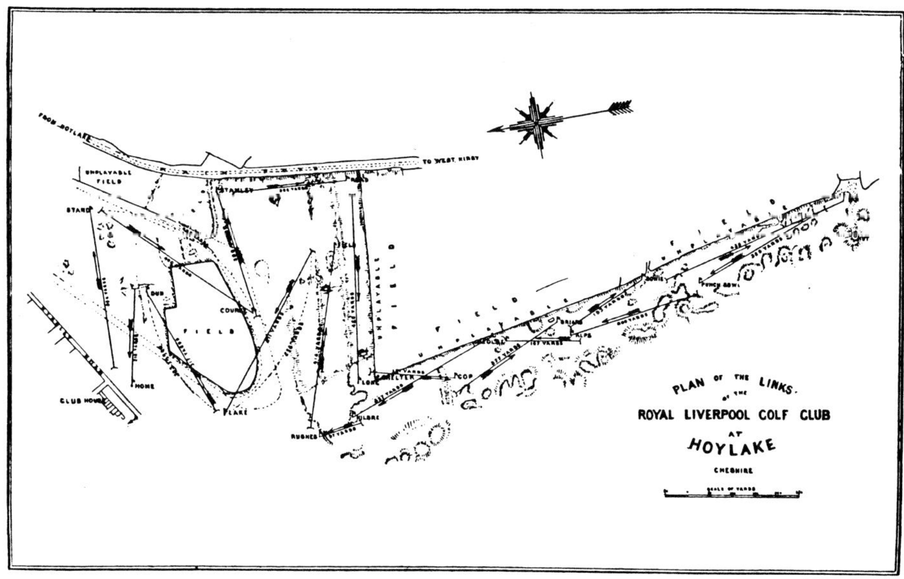

Plan of Hoylake from *The Golfing Annual*, 1888

All good golf links are at the mouth of a river; and this is true of Hoylake, only more so, for it is at the mouth of two. Links ground — i.e. ground with a sandy subsoil, which is the only soil on which the real game of golf can be played — is the work of alluvial deposit. The river brings down the crude material for bunkers; the sea, washing in, arrests it; so that gradually it reclaims itself, and a short close grass grows over it to make it a golf links.

The remark that the golfer will be inclined to make on his first view of Hoylake links will be uncomplimentary. It is so flat. It looks as if it were going to be uninteresting. But it is not so. It has corners of fields which stick out in unexpected and cunningly vexatious places; it has 'cops', which is North-country English for banks; and it has ditches. Then on the Dee-side of the course there are great sandhills almost rivalling the majesty of the Prestwick Himalayas; and the whole length and breadth of the course is the arena of a struggle for existence between the alien golfer and the native rabbit. The place used to be called the Rabbit Warren ... It sounds ominous. Even today at Hoylake it is quite curious, considering how difficult it is to get a ball into a golf hole, how easy it is to get it into a rabbit hole, and this in the days when the golfer has got the upper hand, and driven the rabbit into the skirts of the course — his 'Reserves' ... But Ole Brer Rabbit is less bold and ubiquitous than he used to be, and another form of vexation is quickly disappearing in the posts and rails of the old disused racecourse. The golfer's wrath and niblick and the people's need of firewood have almost made an end of them.

The article continues with a description of the holes and how they might be played. With most of the trouble, to the left — cops and unplayable fields on the way out, and the benty sandhills on the first few holes home, the writer suggests 'on the whole it is better at Hoylake to be on the heel than on the pull'. Playing the last few holes one is back amongst the rabbits' Reserves. 'No wild driver', he adds, 'should come to Hoylake without a ferret trained to draw gutta-percha.'

And so back to the Royal green in front of the hotel for lunch— 'Hoylake is also famous for its shrimps and prawns. Its potted shrimps are almost better than its putting greens.'

Johnny was the firm favourite to win the Championship for the second time, and his play in the earlier rounds confirmed the predictions. Having won the first two games by wide margins, he faced a fellow club member, the young and fast improving Harold Hilton, in the quarter finals. A large crowd enjoyed what was at first a close and exciting match. At the halfway stage they were level but the game turned against Hilton at the 15th and 16th both of which he lost to give Johnny a 3 and 2 victory and his appointed place in the semi-final.

Johnny's play next morning against Leslie Balfour was only moderate. But, reaching the turn in 43 shots, he stood 3 up and 'this advantage Mr Ball took very good care to keep; Mr Balfour was playing a losing game.' The other semi-final was won by Johnny Laidlay at the Home green and so for the third consecutive year the two great rivals battled it out for the medals. As already recounted, at Prestwick two years earlier, Laidlay had fallen to Ball in the final. Next year he had gained his revenge at St Andrews after a thrilling semi-final match ended at the 20th hole with Johnny's seemingly perfect second shot with a cleek running past the pin and into

Ball putting in a match against Laidlay

the pot bunker beyond.

Laidlay was a year older than Ball and he too had developed his skills at an early age. During term time at Loretto he played on the Musselburgh links which he had holed in 36 shots at the age of 16, a remarkable feat when one looks at the Open Championship scores there in the 1880s. In the holidays he played at North Berwick, sometimes four rounds in a day. Soon he was starting his collection of medals from all the leading Clubs—the Royal & Ancient, the Honourable Company, Tantallon, Luffness—not to mention some successes at Hoylake too. In length and accuracy with the wooden clubs and cleek he could not match Ball, but the quality of his short game and an excellent temperament enabled him to achieve the results which justified the claim that he was at that time Scotland's leading amateur player.

So to the final. The start was delayed by a thunderstorm, but when they set off they were 'accompanied by a larger crowd than ever, and though the rain came down again in occasional torrents, it could not damp the ardour of the spectators, who tramped every inch of the round with undiminished interest to the exciting end.'

Johnny drew first blood with a putt for a 4 at the opening hole against Laidlay's 5, and 'the latter lost himself the next hole through taking a bad line with his second. He lost the distance through carrying into the forbidden ground and although he did finish with a 6 with a fine putt he had played 3 more, and Mr Ball had only to hole out to win.' With a half in 3 at the Stanley and another 3 at the Road Johnny became 3 up. Another half (in 6) at the Long was followed by a run of 4s to the turn at which point, out in 37, he was 6 up. Thereafter Laidlay played well but could do no more than win the Meols and the Rushes and the end came at the next hole — 4 up and 3 to play. With a steady finish of one 5 and two 4s, each of them could have completed the round in under 80, 76 for Ball and 79 for Laidlay. As for the crowd: 'the pent up enthusiasm of the natives at once found full vent, and amidst round upon round of hearty cheering, the winner was hoisted onto willing shoulders, which bore him in gratified triumph from the Links to the Club room of the Royal Liverpool.'

Johnny Laidlay

The second major event of the year, the Open Championship, was to be played in September at Prestwick. In the earlier part of the month the interest of the golfing press was centred on

Andrew Kirkaldy

Willie Park Junior, 1890

a £100 challenge match over four greens, 36 holes at each, between Andrew Kirkaldy of St Andrews and young Willie Park of Musselburgh. They had tied for the Open Championship the previous year at Musselburgh and the home player had won the play off. Just before this year's Championship the final 36 holes were played at St Andrews. Crowds were reported to be between 4,000 and 5,000, maybe because their local man was in the lead. He duly won by 8 and 7. Thus the clear favourite amongst the forty golfers who gathered at Prestwick for the Championship was Andrew Kirkaldy. Some however fancied Willie Park to win again, and of the other professionals Fernie and Simpson were expected to do well. Only Douglas Rolland of the leading players was absent. It was agreed that one or two of the amateurs, Ball, Laidlay, Hutchinson and Leitch might also be seen in contention.

The *Saturday Review* description of the links is reproduced in the Appendix. The prospect of disaster in the depths of the Cardinal's Bunker, or the Pow Burn, at the foothills of the Himalayas, or on the dreaded Railway, will have caused more apprehension to the professional in 1890 with gutty ball, than it does to the members of Prestwick today.

The Championship started with near gale force winds from the north west buffeting the early competitors and encouraging them to take a cautious line away from the railway from the 1st tee. Ben Sayers and Willie Park were amongst the early starters and both suffered in the high winds. As the winds moderated later in the morning it favoured those at the rear of the field—Archie Simpson, Andrew and Hugh Kirkaldy and Johnny and his playing partner Willie Campbell. Campbell was professional from Bridge of Weir and had finished runner up in the Championship once and third on two occasions. This was the game that the majority of the crowd decided to follow, and they were not disappointed though it was the young amateur that gave them more to applaud.

Ben Sayers, 1890

After 18 holes Andrew Kirkaldy led with an 81; his brother Hugh was tied with Johnny on 82 and Archie Simpson was a stroke behind. Willie Fernie, who was one of the earlier starters and had scored 85 in the worst of the weather and David Brown with the same score were the only others thought to have a chance.

It was Fernie who set the target, and, with an 82 in the second round, his total was 167. Hugh Kirkaldy who was playing with Simpson was twice on the Railway to take 7 at the Cemetery (1st hole) and with another 7 at the Cardinal he was quickly out of the picture. The 8th and 9th holes (Monkton and the End hole) were the crucial ones. Just at the time that Andrew Kirkaldy was taking 7 at the 9th Johnny was in trouble at Monkton. Up till that point he had played steadily dropping only two strokes.

> *A little variety was imparted to the game at Monkton when playing his second Mr Ball was unfortunate enough to carry into the Railway. For some time the ball could not be found and it seemed as though the player was to lose the distance as well as the stroke, but a diligent search was instituted and the ball was at length discovered. This saved Mr Ball the distance. He dropped the ball and playing 4 got down in 6. A 5 at the End hole saw him out in 41.*

At this stage he stood one stroke ahead of Simpson who despite a 7 at the Cardinal had also completed the first nine holes in 41, and two ahead of Andrew Kirkaldy; of the latter: 'those that remained with the St Andrews man did not see him at his best. He would have to improve much if he was to stand well in, but he began the homeward journey with a 5 and 5s continued to be the order of the day with him all through the second half.' Meanwhile Archie Simpson was also dropping a stroke or two and could only equal Fernie's target of 167. So with four holes to play Johnny had only to complete them in 20 strokes. By this time the bulk of the crowd was following him and no doubt the adrenalin was flowing as it does with the scent of victory. The quality of his long game was maintained and even his putting which had let him down earlier in the day became more accurate; two 5s and two 4s saw him safely home to win by three strokes from Archie Simpson and Willie Fernie.

His figures for the two rounds were:

First round	*Out*	*5, 3, 5, 4, 4, 6, 3, 5, 6 = 41*
	Home	*5, 5, 4, 5, 4, 6, 5, 4, 3 = 41 = 82*
Second round	*Out*	*4, 4, 5, 5, 4, 4, 4, 6, 5 = 41*
	Home	*5, 5, 5, 4, 4, 5, 4, 5, 4 = 41 = 82*

To quote from the *Scottish Observer* 'They were characterised by extraordinary steadiness and brilliancy combined.' *The Field* spoke of his driving: 'full of fire and straight as an arrow, while his uniformly good approach play never left him too much to do on the putting green' and *Golf* (26 September edition) of his style and temperament:

> *The victory of Mr Ball is a very popular one and is recognised even by the professionals themselves as having been no fluke but as being on the contrary the outcome of commanding superiority over all his competitors. Mr Ball's style of play was very much admired by all who witnessed it; and his unassuming demeanour throughtout presented an admirable example of what all successful golfers ought to be. He possesses in an eminent degree, too, the faculty of being wholly absorbed in the game to the exclusion of all outside influences. We have never seen a more imperturbable player —a player who was so little affected by the casual movements of spectators, or other like small disturbances. In this respect his behaviour through the Links was in striking contrast with that of some professional players of high rank. Willie Park and Archie Simpson are the two professionals most like the Champion in their indifference to what is going on around them.*

The Double Champion

Whether it was modesty, caution or cunning the story is told that before the Championship started he had a bet on himself to win £2, and then hedged with 30 shillings on other leading contenders. Thus he won the princely sum of 10 shillings to go with the gold medal, which still rests proudly in the showcase at Hoylake alongside the Amateur Championship medal which he had won four months earlier. For the first time the cup was to leave Scotland. An Englishman and an amateur had beaten the full army of Scottish professionals. This was without doubt a momentous year in the development of the Open Championship and in the growth of golf south of the border.

Back at Hoylake a celebratory dinner was held at which after speeches of congratulation a new rendering of John Peel was sung with the refrain:

Yes we ken John Ball and his modesty too,
His skillful play and his heart so true
And his Champion score of twice eighty two
On Prestwick Links in the morning.

A few weeks later at the end of January 1891 at the annual general meeting of the club he was elected a life member recorded in the minutes in the following manner:

The Chairman said that since the last Annual Meeting one of our members Mr John Ball Junior had performed a feat hitherto unparalleled in the annals of golf by not only winning the Amateur Championship which was in itself a great victory but also beating allcomers at Prestwick in the Open Championship. He felt sure that the proposal he was about to make, which he did with the full consent of Council, would be received with acclamation by those present. He then proposed that Mr John Ball Junior be made a life member of the Royal Liverpool Golf Club in remembrance of the great victory he had gained, which had not only reflected glory on himself but also on the Club with which his name was so intimately connected. This was seconded by Mr R.W. Brown and carried unanimously.

And doubtless received with the appropriate acclamation.

The Open and Amateur Championship medals won by John Ball

6 — The Title Defences (1891 - 1892)

The lifestyle of an Open Champion one hundred years ago was very different from today. For Johnny, once the euphoria and celebrations were over, it was back to routines. He still lived with family at the Royal Hotel, helping as required there and working on his farm down Meols Drive.

> *Far from sacrificing everything to golf, as a player of such calibre might perhaps be excused for doing, he is, so say his friends, often reluctantly and with difficulty persuaded to play, nor does he ever sacrifice his business on his farm (which by the way is very successful) for the sake of a match. Probably on this account he plays all the better, and on one occasion some two years ago, he sowed with his own hand an eight acre field of oats on the day previous to an important match; and so far was this from prejudicially affecting his game, that when he came to play he holed the round in 76. An early riser, he has been known to spend a morning on a hayrick working like a nigger (pretty hard work this in sultry weather) appearing anon as fresh as paint for a big match in the afternoon.*

Nor was golf his only sporting skill; he excelled at shooting 'as the rabbits on Hoylake Golf Course could testify', horse riding, ice skating and most notably as an athlete, where he could give a start of a yard or two in a hundred to any local over the hurdles or on the flat.

Both the Amateur and Open Championships of 1891 were to be held on the Old Course at St Andrews, a links which had not yet seen the best of Ball. Johnny, as he often seemed to do, showed fine early season form, winning the Easter competition with a 76 plus 8 and the Club Gold Medal at the Spring Meeting with an 82. However on the second day he took 91: 'He was off his game with a severe cold and sore throat.' Perhaps he had not fully recovered when he reached St Andrews for the Amateur Championship a few days later, for he struggled through the first round with a last green victory against J. Kirk from Glasgow, a much older player, and then, despite recovering from 3 down with 6 to play against another outsider, R.B. Sharp from Dundee, he 'lost his head at the last hole'; his third shot, a running pitch through the Valley of Sin, just made it to the top but he putted 4 feet short and missed to allow Sharp a win in 5. The Hoylake flag however remained flying to the end with Harold Hilton reaching his first final. Johnny Laidlay, there for the fourth time, was his opponent. Hilton had looked the winner at the 19th hole, but Laidlay scrambled a half from the left of the green and won at the 20th to become Amateur Champion for the second time.

Soon after Johnny's return from St Andrews he made a further trip to Sandwich and won the St George's Grand Challenge Cup for the fourth time—each year since its inception in 1888. This event had become the premier stroke play tournament in England, and many of the top amateurs participated, attracted in part by the valuable prize—a replica of the £400 Gold Cup.

Thereafter there is little evidence from competition results of him playing much golf that summer; perhaps this was due to his work on the farm or to his

MR. HAROLD H. HILTON.

involvement with the formation of a new club at Leasowe. Whilst it has been suggested that Leasowe was founded by Hoylake golfers dissatisfied that play there was not permitted on Sundays, it was in fact started with a 9 hole layout on Leasowe Common, near to the old Moreton lighthouse, with play restricted to Saturdays. At first, before a club house was erected, Mrs Williams the lighthouse keeper provided tea and buns for the members. Johnny still only 29, became their first captain, an office which he was to hold for four years, and he played regularly there, winning competitions from time to time despite a handicap of plus 10. After two years, play on the original course was abandoned due to 'disturbances on the links', and nearly twelve months elapsed before competitions were resumed on some new land by the castle. The Moreton Ladies took over the old clubhouse, and their club thrived on the Common for a number of years.

On moving to the new course it seems that play did take place on Sundays because in 1898 a special general meeting was held to introduce a rule change 'that no golf be played on Leasowe Green on Sundays'. Johnny spoke for the motion.

> *He said that having been connected with the Green Committee from the formation of the Club, and Chairman for some four years, as such he might be expected to know something about the nature of the Leasowe turf. He went on to state that in his opinion if play were allowed on Sunday it would be more than the course could stand and that in a very short time the links would not be worth playing on. He further stated that it must be remembered that in playing 18 holes on a 9 hole course the same ground was played over twice, thus giving the ground double the amount of wear that would appear at first sight.*

The motion required a two-thirds majority, and was carried by the narrowest possible margin — 82 votes to 41.

The other special feature of Leasowe is that it has never opened its doors to the fair sex—though they did get better treatment than dogs — as an early Rule Book tells . 'No dog shall be allowed within the Club house or on the ground, and any member bringing same will be liable to a fine of 1/-.'

The Open Championship for 1891 was to be held on 6 October but this was not announced by the Royal & Ancient Golf Club until the beginning of September, a mere month's notice, which elicited the following letter from Potter, the Royal Liverpool secretary, to the R & A secretary.

4th September 1891

My dear Grace,
I see by yesterday's Scotsman that the Open Championship is fixed for the 6th October ... It was fully John Ball junior's intention to have another battle for the Championship honours but you having clashed with our Autumn Meeting week, it is very doubtful if you will see him at St Andrews this year; do not you think these important fixtures could be settled earlier in the year and advertised so that other Clubs could make arrangements accordingly? ... With kind regards. T.O. Potter

The Royal Liverpool Autumn Meeting dates of 7 and 9 October had been advertised since the beginning of the year. Grace obviously replied in conciliatory terms and a further letter was despatched by Potter to Grace on 9 September.

My dear Grace,
Thank you very much for your letter of yesterday just received; I think if the date could be altered it would certainly be desirable. The 26th September will suit John Ball junior and to this effect I wired you this afternoon guessing that my letter would not reach you in time for your meeting tomorrow the result of which will you kindly let me know. On reference I see 6th October clashes also with the Royal North Devon Autumn Meeting. If at your meeting tomorrow, the 26th September be accepted you can easily telegraph the alteration to The Field etc. I will send you the Cup next week under advice and thanking you for the trouble you have taken in the matter believe me. Yours sincerely, T.O. Potter.

In the event the meeting confirmed the original date, so sadly it is not possible to record that the date of the Open Championship was altered to avoid a clash with a Royal Liverpool club medal.

Johnny's success in 1890 had the effect of encouraging more amateurs to participate, and of making the professionals all the keener to wrest back the trophy. Thus a field of 83, 43 professionals and 40 amateurs, assembled for a 9 am start on 6 October in a southerly gale and squally showers. Johnny was again paired with Campbell from Bridge of Weir; again they took a large crowd, and with 41 to the turn it seemed that he was carrying on where he had left off at Prestwick. However a series of mishaps on the homeward holes, made more difficult by the strong wind, culminated in disaster when 'he threw himself out of contention at the last green but one. A long brassie shot carried him over the road into a ditch where be lay so badly that after a couple of indifferent attempts to extricate himself he was compelled to lift and lose a couple of strokes.'

It all added up to 94, the same score as Campbell. With the pressure off in the second round he returned an 83, which equalled the lowest afternoon score, done by Hugh Kirkaldy, who became the new Champion.

Johnny had no intention of missing the first day of Hoylake's Autumn Meeting the following day and so, after completing his second round, he headed south. He was doubtless in the company of Harold Hilton who had finished second amateur a few strokes ahead of him, and their friend Willie More formerly a member of Royal Liverpool but now professional at Chester who had taken fifth prize. It seems unlikely, with the large field, and a late starting time, that he could have finished in time to catch the train from St Andrews at 5.30 pm, which would have enabled him to return home via Perth and Carlisle. The alternative routing, leaving St Andrews at 7.15 pm involved six changes and 14 hours of travel. For the record this is the routing:

St Andrews	*Depart 7.15 pm*	
Leuchars Junction	*Arrive 7.27 pm*	*(Change)*
Leuchars Junction	*Depart 7.41 pm*	
Edinburgh Waverley	*Arrive 9.05 pm*	*(Change)*
Edinburgh Waverley	*Depart 9.30 pm*	
York	*Arrive 2.15 am*	*(Change)*
York	*Depart 3.55 am*	
Leeds New	*Arrive 4.35 am*	*(Change station)*
Leeds (Central)	*Depart 5.00 am*	
Manchester Victoria	*Arrive 6.40 am*	*(Change)*
Manchester Victoria	*Depart 6.50 am*	
Liverpool Exchange	*Arrive 8.45 am*	*(Change station)*
Liverpool James St	*Depart 9.05 am*	
Hoylake	*Arrive 9.38 am*	

The good news was that the strong wind at Hoylake in the morning moderated as the day advanced and, with late starting times, the weary travellers took the Dowie Cup and Hall Blyth medals, the first and second scratch prizes. Johnny won the former with an 82 to Harold Hilton's 87.

1892 was another year of great achievement for Royal Liverpool and its two crack players. New venues had been chosen for the two premier events. The Amateur was to be staged at St George's, Sandwich, and the Open at Muirfield, the new home of the Honourable Company of Edinburgh Golfers. The course and clubhouse had been completed only in December, though 16 of the holes had been open for play for more than 12 months. Another major change had been agreed in that it was to be contested over four rounds and two days. This did not go as far as Mr H.S.C. Everard had suggested in the columns of the *National Observer* the previous year. His proposal to find the true champion golfer was that 36 holes Medal should be played and the leading eight would qualify for all-against-all matchplay over 18 holes. Nine rounds in five days would therefore be required to find the winner. His other plea that the miserably inadequate prizes should be increased was, however, heeded and the winner, if a professional, was now to receive £35.

Despite the inaccessibility of Sandwich, particularly for the Scots, the entry for the Amateur Championship was 45, nearly half of whom had entered from clubs north of the border. One of the leading Scottish players, Andy Stuart, was Johnny's first opponent. It looked likely that this first round would be his last as he was 4 down at the 10th hole and had missed his second shot to the 11th. Stuart, however, topped into a bunker and lost a hole he should have won, allowing Ball to claw his way back to win at the 18th. More excitement followed with successive games against Mure Fergusson, Horace Hutchinson and Leslie Balfour going all the way or nearly so. Against Fergusson he managed to win on the 17th due to a missed short putt: 'The effort being certainly not helped by the click of a photographic apparatus, which articles were numerous on the ground and were a source of terror to the more nervous players.'

Meanwhile Hilton was cruising to the final by means of an easier draw and some excellent play which enabled him to beat Laidlay in the semi-final by 5 and 4. After 12 holes of the final the match was square, but Johnny holed a good putt at the 13th to take the lead. The 14th was crucial. In Hilton's words:

To the fourteenth I had the best of the wooden club play, my second being quite close to the bunker guarding the green, whilst his was some way short, and as the approach was down wind and the green keen, I had a distinct advantage. His approach was not a good one; it was far too merry and looked like finishing in the rushes beyond the green, but it struck the guiding post on the far edge of the green and bounced back. My third finished some seven or eight yards past the pin. His run up was played beautifully and he nearly holed it, the ball finishing about a foot past the hole. Now my approach putt had to be played on a slippery green ...

Amateur Championship 1892 from the *Illustrated Sporting and Dramatic News*

Yes, you have guessed, Hilton left it short and missed the next one to go 2 down. Two holes later Johnny had become Champion for the third time.

Undoubtedly Hilton had played the best golf through the Championship and he always considered 'that this was the only final I ever played in which fortune was a little unkind to me'. In *The Field* report however it suggested that Hilton 'was hardly playing so well as in the morning'.

An interesting match took place during the meeting when the two Hoylake amateurs played a 36 hole foursome against Hugh Kirkaldy (the Open Champion) and Douglas Rolland. Although Rolland was driving the ball as well as he had been in his match against Johnny ten years earlier — distances up to 250 yards — the amateurs gained a notable win on the 35th green.

Muirfield for the Open Championship was a very different test — shorter, more lush and less sandy than most of the other links courses. For some reason it seemed to suit the amateurs better than the professionals. Horace Hutchinson was to regret the fact that the Championship had been extended to 72 holes, for he led the field by three shots at the end of the first day with a score of 152. Park, Herd and Johnny were three shots behind, and Hilton in seventh place six shots adrift. Next morning the two Hoylake amateurs were in fine form, Ball with a 74 and Hilton 72 and so with eighteen holes to play a leader board would have showed:

Mr John Ball junior	*229*
Mr Harold Hilton	*231*
Sandy Herd	*232*
Hugh Kirkaldy	*233*
James Kay	*234*
Willie Park junior	*235*

The two Hoylake Champions

Horace Hutchinson had faded from the picture with a disastrous 86.

For the final round Johnny was near the front of the field and was thus setting the target. His driving and second shots were as good as ever 'but his short game left room for slight improvement and several times the ball stopped short'. It was an uninspired round - all 5s and 4s until a 3 at the 17th hole. The total was 79 and the target 308. Both Kirkaldy and Herd had seemed likely to beat that score, but each took a 6 at the 18th to join Johnny as joint leaders, thus leaving the way open to Harold Hilton. He duly capitalised on his good fortune in holing two approach shots in the first nine holes and came in with a 74 and three shots to spare.

Although after three rounds it had looked as though Johnny might repeat his 1890 achievement it was not to be; but for Hoylake, with the winner and runner-up in the two major Championships of the year, it was a double double.

Johnny — recovering from the Maiden

7 — Success and Failure (1893 - 1895)

Following the first Amateur won by Allan Macfie the Championship had been dominated by the three leading amateurs — Ball, Laidlay and Hutchinson for the next seven years. In 1891 and 1892 Hilton had given notice of intent, but the man to break the monopoly in 1893 was P.C. Anderson from St Andrews University, who beat Laidlay, playing in his fifth final in six years. The most significant event in that Championship, however, was the emergence of the young Scottish lion Freddie Tait, who was to figure prominently in forthcoming events.

Freddie Tait driving

Mure Fergusson

Freddie was the son of Professor Tait of Edinburgh, who was more noted for his theories on the game than the practice of it. He was educated at Sedbergh, Edinburgh University and Sandhurst, being commissioned in 1890, and was an outstanding sportsman reaching a high standard at rugby, cricket and shooting as well as golf. It was his personality, however, that captivated all around him — strong, good-looking, high-spirited but deeply caring and devoid of conceit. This all combined to win him many admirers, not just fellow golfers and soldiers but the Scottish public with whom admiration turned to hero worship. So with Hilton and Tait now on the scene, the old guard would need to look to their laurels.

This was just what Johnny did in the 1894 Championship, back at Hoylake again. He was at his best and reached the semi-final with a series of crushing victories, to be joined there by Laidlay, Tait and Mure Fergusson. Johnny beat his old rival Laidlay with something to spare and waited for the outcome of the other match, anticipating a first contest with the young pretender. Tait however played poorly and it was the senior Scotsman who won the other place in the final, the man who had beaten Ball in the previous year's Championship. As had happened in 1890, the start was delayed by heavy rain but this did not deter the vast crowd, bigger than those seen in Scotland and estimated at about 4,000. The finalists were continually required 'to drive down a living lane of humanity'. Johnny took the first four holes, but once a large lead begins to evaporate tension creeps into the game. So, with two holes left to play, the match was back to all square and thoughts of the previous year's defeat were doubtless in Johnny's mind. The Scottish supporters were in full cry: 'Johnny Ball's beaten — he's funking.' This however was the moment for one of his great strokes — a stroke that is remembered at Hoylake alongside Roberto's famous second shot three-quarters of a century later. That second shot at the Dun hole at this time had to be played with the Field intruding on the right, and, if the green was to be reached, over a fearsome cross-bunker. Mure Fergusson had played short, but Johnny, taking courage in his hands, went for the green with his favourite brassie. The ball soared over the Field, carried the cross-bunker and ran to within 10 yards of the pin. This was the shot that won him his fourth championship.

Mure Fergusson was clearly upset both by the crowd control, and by the poor press comment relating to his play in the final and he made his feelings known through a letter to the editor of *Golf:*

> *Sir,*
> *I amused myself yesterday by reading extracts from different papers on the final heat for the Amateur Championship, and among other accounts I read that of Mr Horace Hutchinson in your paper. I am surprised he should take so much pains to point out that he thought the play, especially on my part, so inferior. But I doubt, even if Mr Horace Hutchinson had played instead of me, whether he would have been able to pull out his true form. He seems to ignore the fact of our having to drive off the tee down a lane of people, having a feeling all the time that one would probably injure someone, which is not calculated to make one drive well and thus affects the whole part of the game. The approach shots also were very difficult to play, caused by the difficulty in determining the distance, owing to the deep crowds standing at the back of the hole. I fancy I am not singular in my view, that as a rule a match of this sort is not calculated to produce low scoring ... As Mr Horace Hutchinson has played so often in these sort of contests, I think he should extend a little more charity to those not so successful as himself trying to win first honours. Apologising for the length of this letter I am Sir etc. S. Mure Fergusson.*

It was not Johnny's only victory of that year. The previous year he had played for the first time in the Irish Championship, and won it. Thus he went to defend his title at Dollymount and won again, beating D.L. Low by 9 and 7 in the final. Four times he played in this Championship and won three of them. The other he lost in an early round to a 17-year-old, and his generosity in defeat gained him as many friends as had all his victories.

A story is told of his third victory, which shows that there was a hard streak in him — when he wanted to show it. This was a few years later at Portmarnock where he was due to play in the final against a good golfer from Edinburgh with a notoriously bad temper.

> *The night before the Secretary told Ball not to turn up at 10 o'clock which was the advertised starting time, but to be ready to start at 10.30 as he had a professional competition to get off before the final. Unfortunately the wretched Secretary forgot to*

tell the other man and got his professionals off much quicker than he expected and, when Johnny arrived at about ten minutes past ten he heard an awful noise on the first tee and came to see what was happening. The man was cursing the Secretary and then turned on Johnny saying that he ought to be disqualified. 'Hold hard you can't do that to me, I'm here well before the time I was told and anyhow we have all day to play thirty six holes.' The man said 'Oh no I want to get the match over early to catch the evening boat back to Scotland.' Johnny replied 'All right I won't keep you long just let me change my shoes.' He won 13 up and 11 to play, made the man a little bow and said 'Now Sir you can catch your boat.'

The two victories in 1894 were just oases in the desert of a long hard season. The time pressures on the top amateur golfers can be illustrated by a reconstruction of Johnny's golfing tournament programme for the year. After a few excursions in Winter Optional Handicap Sweepstakes at Hoylake in the first three months, it began in earnest at Lytham:

7 April	*Lytham Spring Meeting 1st day — 82 — tied for Clifton scratch medal with Hilton. Won play-off with 83*
9 April	*Lytham Spring Meeting 2nd day — 85 + 9 = 94. Second to Hilton for Ladies scratch medal.*
14 April	*Bowdon (near Manchester) Open Scratch Meeting — tied second with an 87. Won by Hilton.*
23 April	*Royal Liverpool Spring Meeting 1st day — 84. Second to Hutchinson and wins Dun Silver Cross.*
24 April	*Royal Liverpool Spring Meeting 2nd day — 83. Second to Laidlay and wins Stanley of Alderley gold medal. Plays challenge match in afternoon with Laidlay against Hutchinson and Hutchings and wins 1 up.*
25 April	*Amateur Championship begins at Hoylake. 1st round beats Goldie (Airdrie) by 7 and 6 and 2nd round Pease (Alnmouth) by 6 and 4.*
26 April	*3rd and 4th rounds of the Championship — beats Fairclough (Royal Liverpool) 5 and 4 and Gray (Musselburgh) 6 and 5.*
27 April	*Semi-final—beats Laidlay 5 and 3 and Mure Fergusson by 1 hole in final.*
5 May	*am Royal Liverpool monthly medal — 83 + 9 = 92;* *pm Exhibition match to open new links at Leasowe.*
23 May	*Practice round at Windermere prior to Grand Amateur Tournament—round in 70. Course record.*
25 May	*Windermere Grand Amateur Scratch Prize — 73 + 76 = 149. Second to Hilton.*
26 May	*Windermere handicap cup — 77 + 81 = 158 + 18 = 176.*
2 June	*Royal Liverpool monthly medal — 83 + 9 = 92.*
11 June	*Open Championship at Sandwich 1st and 2nd rounds — 84 + 89.*
12 June	*Open Championship 3rd and 4th rounds — 87 + 84 for a total of 344. Tied for 13th place.*

13 June	*St George's Grand Challenge Cup — 88 + 86 — fifth place. Won by Hilton.*
14 June	*Professional and Amateur Matchplay Tournament at Sandwich — beats Willie Park by 1 hole, but loses to J.H. Taylor by 4 and 3.*

The call of haymaking and other duties on the farm may have filled the next few weeks as there is no record of any further competitive play until early August. It started again with a further trip to Lytham:

4 August	*Lytham Summer Meeting (Silver Iron) — 86 + 86 = 172. Second to Hilton.*
6 August	*Royal Liverpool Summer Meeting — 89 + 9 = 98.*
11 August	*Leasowe Summer Meeting — 71 + 10 = 81.*
18 August	*Leasowe Medal — 77 + 10 = 87.*
31 August	*Two rounds with W.D. More, professional from Chester, at Hoylake. 2nd round in 74 - a record.*
4 September	*Dollymount Open Handicap competition — 75 + 4 = 79. Second place.*
5 September	*Irish Championship at Dollymount — 2nd and 3rd rounds. Beat Herdman (Royal Belfast) 9 and 7 and J. Taylor (Carlton) 1 hole.*
6 September	*4th round and semi-final — beat Young (Monifieth) 3 and 2 and Henderson (Edinburgh University) 4 and 2.*
7 September	*Final over 36 holes — beat Low (Monifieth) by 9 and 7. Then played exhibition match with H. Kirkaldy. Won 1 up.*
8 September	*Professional and amateur strokeplay event at Dollymount — 81 + 84 = 165. Finished 6th.*

And then back home for the harvesting, before the autumn circuit began:

3 October	*Royal Liverpool Autumn Meeting 1st day — 87 + 9 = 96. Scratch medal won by Hilton.*
5 October	*Royal Liverpool Autumn Meeting 2nd day — 83 + 9 = 92. Scratch medal won by Hutchinson.*
13 October	*Lytham Autumn Meeting 1st day — 82 + 9 = 91. Wins Manchester scratch medal.*
15 October	*Lytham Autumn Meeting 2nd day — 76 + 9 = 85. A record score and wins Thistleton scratch medal.*
20 October	*Leasowe — round in 70 in friendly game — course record.*
1 November	*St David's Golf Club, Harlech Open Meeting — 75 + 77 = 152. Wins scratch bowl.*
2 November	*St David's Golf Club Handicap prize — 77 + 72 = 149 + 18 = 167. Second round a course record and wins second prize.*

In the last two months there were a few more local competitions, including the St Andrews Meeting at Hoylake, where Johnny won the Milligan gold medal.

So the year ended for him with two Championship cups, five course records, and a handful of scratch medals. Despite this *The Golfing Annual* review placed Tait, who was carrying all before him in Scotland, as 'first of the Amateurs today'. Perhaps this was justified for Johnny's stroke play results were inconsistent, and as we have seen Hilton frequently finished ahead of him in the quest for medals in club and open events.

If 1894 was to be remembered by Johnny for his famous shot at the Dun hole in the Amateur Championship final, in 1895 there was another shot — not so famous — which will surely have haunted him for a month or two.

The Amateur Championship was at St Andrews and with a kind draw Johnny yet again reached the semi-final where he was to play his first Championship match against Freddie Tait. Harold Hilton, eliminated in earlier rounds, was a spectator and he described the build up to this game.

> *There was a delightful international flavour about the meeting of these two; they represented the respective hopes of Scotland and England, and moreover there was more than a little wagering on the result. The Scotsmen not only pinned their faith to Freddie Tait on account of his golfing ability; they argued to themselves that in the first place he was playing over his home green, to which he had always evinced a strong partiality, whilst in the second his enemy had never done well over the classic green, nor shown any strong liking for its peculiarities; and these little facts seemed to turn the balance in favour of the local man. Well, Freddie did not win, and moreover did not win a single hole.*

He had missed a short putt on the first hole and thereafter looked and played as a beaten man.

The opponent in the final was Leslie Balfour Melville, a member of the Royal and Ancient of 20 years standing, a successful Edinburgh lawyer and another sportsman of great distinction. He represented Scotland at both rugby football and cricket and won the Lawn Tennis Championship of Scotland. Not surprisingly, the crowd having seen their first favourite beaten transferred their partisan affections to him.

It was a fluctuating match. Johnny had won the first three holes but the luck had turned against him and he came to the 17th hole dormie two down. He was not done, however, and with a 5 and a 4 he squared the game. So for the third successive round Balfour Melville went to the 19th. Both Greig and Auchterlonie had obligingly put their second shots in the burn in the preceding rounds. The wind had now changed and this time both players played short with their second. Balfour Melville was safely on for three; Johnny took out his pitching mashie, a club he hardly ever used, preferring the straight-faced clubs where possible, and, amidst muffled groans from the English supporters and yells of excitement from the Scots, the ball lobbed into the burn and disappeared with a fatal splash—together with his hopes of victory.

As for the unruly behaviour of the crowds this was nicely summarised in *The Scotsman:* 'The glorious reception he [Johnny] received on presentation of his prize more than testified any display of feeling during the game was very far indeed from being directed against him personally. I'm afraid the truth may be that we Scots are an excitable lot. Personally I blame the porridge and oatcakes not the whisky.'

Leslie Balfour Melville on the Old course, St Andrews

The first four Amateur Champions: Laidlay, Ball, Hutchinson and Anderson

8 — Ball *v* Tait (1896–1899)

'The faculty of golf ebbs and flows like the tides of the sea.' So said Horace Hutchinson in the *National Observer Golf Review* after one of John Ball's less than prolific years. The tide was certainly out by his own standard for the years of 1896, 1897 and 1898. In those three Amateur Championships he reached the quarter-final twice, losing to Tait in 1896 and Robb in 1898, and, in the year between, failed at the first attempt after an epic encounter with Robert Maxwell involving five extra holes of the highest quality golf. As for the Open he competed only in 1897 when he finished down the field. Back at Hoylake, he did win a few more scratch medals and achieved a new course record of 76 in October 1896. It was however Harold Hilton's name that was now seen more frequently in the top position. How can one explain this barren period? There was a press report in March 1896 that 'He had the misfortune to strain the muscles of his hand through falling when jumping. A rather serious view was taken of the injury at first but the injured hand is progressing favourably.' Could this have been a reason? More likely it was just that the appetite for competition had waned a little, sapped perhaps by the old problem with his putting.

A portrait from about 1895

These were none the less heady days at Hoylake. The club had just moved from the Royal Hotel into their imposing premises on Meols Drive. The links too had been extended with the club taking a lease on the land to the south of the cop at the Long hole, to create the Telegraph and Briars holes—the 5th and 6th as we know them today. So by 1897 the total length of the course had been extended to 6,050 yards, a worthy test for the Open Championship which was to be held for the first time at Hoylake that year. It turned out to be an especially memorable occasion, with the victory of Harold Hilton who became Champion for the second time. He beat Braid by a shot, proving that his win at Muirfield was no fluke. Finally, a new star was emerging. John Graham junior, the son of a prominent member, had made the transformation from promising junior to established figure on the amateur scene, with a bronze medal in the 1896 Amateur Championship to show for it.

It was however Freddie Tait who had established himself as the leading amateur. He won the Amateur Championships at Sandwich in 1896 and again in 1898 at Hoylake, where the strains of the bagpipes were heard in the clubhouse the evening before the final, and later that night in Market Street. He didn't win the Open

The 1898 Amateur Championship final — the Royal green

Championship, but he finished each time within two or three shots of the winner, 3rd in 1896 and 1897 and 5th in 1898. From north to south he was winning trophies wherever he went, from gold medals at St Andrews to gold cups at St George's.

There was no immediate change to Johnny's golfing fortunes as 1899 began, and though Prestwick had happy memories for him he will not have had great hopes of success as he travelled north. The Amateur Championship had grown in many ways. For the first time the entry exceeded 100. The press appeared in great numbers; in 1893 the local postmaster and one clerk handled the telegrams, but now there were 11 operators called in from Glasgow. A dozen police were brought from nearby stations to help with the crowd control, though in truth 'they were no more effective than the local stewards as they were not familiar with the Royal and Ancient game and they, not the crowds were the offenders'. With the large entry the Championship was well worth winning. The entrance fee of one guinea more than covered the costs, and even with the expenses for extra police (£5), the medals (£14) and advertising (£14) there was £60 left for division between the winner, runner-up and losing semi-finalists. The £30 voucher to the winner equalled the first prize in the previous year's Open Championship, and was quite an increase from the £8 that Johnny had used to purchase his shot gun 11 years earlier.

The week started inauspiciously. In the annual match between Tantallon and Hoylake, the forerunner of the England versus Scotland international match, Ball lost to his old rival Laidlay, and he began the Championship itself with a 50 yard top from the 1st tee. He won the match however and reached the last eight without further anxiety. In this round he played Robert Maxwell again, and, despite an early lead, the match once again went all the way and beyond. A missed 4 foot putt at the 18th might have proved costly, but this time he won at the extra hole. There was no such problem in the afternoon's semi-final. Johnny was at his most brilliant against

Freddie Tait in the 1899 final at Prestwick

the young Prestwick member G.C. Whigham. A score of 35 to the turn put him well ahead and victory came by 8 and 6. Meanwhile Freddie Tait was working his way through the lower half of the draw to reach the final that everyone was hoping for — Scotland versus England, the reigning Champion against the four times winner.

It was just as well that the final was now played over 36 holes for after 14 holes Johnny was 5 down, a deficit he had reduced to 3 by the end of the first round. His putting had been disastrous, and on three occasions he had missed from a couple of feet. The explanation for this putting rings as true today as it did then: 'Mr Ball when he deals with a short putt, does not stand with his body stiff and hit the ball, but he sways his body and gives the ball a push instead of hitting it, and so seems to heel it at one time and draw it at another as the swaying of his body inclines.'

News of the final was telegraphed to the Royal Liverpool Club, the first timed at 11.50 stating tersely 'Tait 5 up at 14th hole' and the second some 40 minutes later: 'Tait 3 up at end of first round.' One wonders if they would have been pasted into the club scrapbook were it not for the events of the second round.

After six holes in the afternoon the match was square again, and Johnny was one ahead by the time he had completed the 14th. 'Ball 1 up at 32nd hole playing splendidly', read the telegram timed at 3.42. He was still one up at Prestwick's famous 17th hole of 378 yards with the blind second shot over the Alps and a deep bunker in front of the green. This bunker was partly flooded. Let Bernard Darwin's *Green Memories* continue the story.

> *My recollection is, that to the historic Alps Mr Tait played the odd, that I felt sure his second was in the bunker, probably in the water and that in my own mind I thought Mr Ball should have played short, and made sure of his 5. No doubt my youthful judgment was wrong. Mr Ball must have come very very near to getting over, and in*

any case I did not make allowances for two things; first that bunkers had no terrors for him; second, that at so tremendous a moment it was the natural and probably the right instinct to go all out to win the match.

In the event Freddie's ball did finish in the water and Johnny's in the sand near the sleepered face. No rule existed then to cover casual water. The ball had to be played as it lay, or as it floated to be more correct. No doubt golfing lawyers of today would have queried whether the ball was moved by the ripples as Freddie waded in to play the shot. Moving or not, he played one of golf's great recovery shots.

The water shot

It was a grand shot, no doubt of that, and as the hero waded out again he was helped up the bank by willing hands, like another Horatio emerging from the Tiber. Long before the cheering had ceased Mr Ball had played an almost equally great shot from horrid hard wet sand with the boarded face close to him. He has however always had a genius all his own for making the ball get up almost vertically if he wants to and out it came apparently with the utmost ease.

The home hole of 252 yards gave both players the hope of a 3 but it was Freddie who achieved it to square the match. Thus, amidst great tension, they went to the Cemetery, as the 1st hole is called.

At this point some of the Hoylake stalwarts could bear it no more and retired to the Clubhouse, where they waited for news, presumably groaning dismally like Mr Winkle with their heads under the sofa cushions. The rest of the world rushed tumultuously out towards the first hole and it became very hard to see anything. This I remember well because when the first ball came pitching onto the green and pitching unluckily, ran over to the far edge, I thought that Mr Ball had probably played the odd and that this was his ball. When the second ball pitched, squirming and screwing its way into the turf, and stopped close to the hole, I thought that all was over. It was quite a perceptible while before my mourning was turned into joy.

It was Johnny who had hit the longer drive and Freddie who had played his second shot first to the back of the green.

Mr Tait had a most difficult approach putt; he hit it extraordinarily well, boldly and truly, and the ball lay as near as might be dead. And then—how long was Mr Ball's putt? and did I actually see him hole it? Honestly I do not know. I should guess that the putt was one of eight feet, and I believe that I saw the ball go in, but could not see the player strike it. At any rate it went in, and the more matches I watch the more I think that this was the greatest, the most prostratingly exciting of them all.

One final message despatched the joyous news to Hoylake: 'Ball won at 37th hole did hole in 3.'

The spirit in which the game was played and the character of Freddie Tait are both portrayed by his comment at the presentation: 'I would rather be beaten by Johnny Ball than by any other man in the world.'

More adulation was to follow when Johnny returned to Hoylake. Crowds five deep on the platform at the station were there to greet him and shake his hand. As he stepped into the waiting carriage he failed to notice that it had been unharnessed,

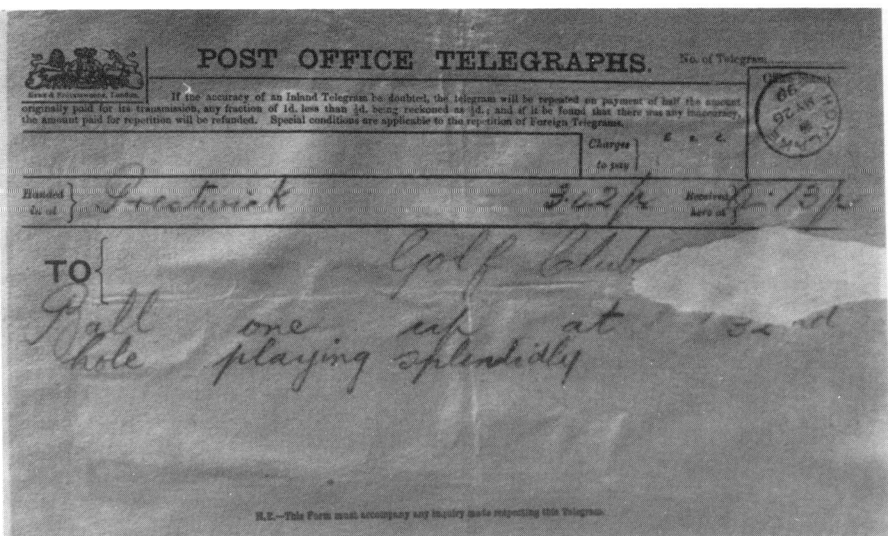

POST OFFICE TELEGRAPHS. No. of Telegram

If the accuracy of an Inland Telegram be doubted, the telegram will be repeated on payment of half the amount originally paid for its transmission, any fraction of 1d. less than ½d. being reckoned as ½d.; and if it be found that there was any inaccuracy, the amount paid for repetition will be refunded. Special conditions are applicable to the repetition of Foreign Telegrams.

Charges to pay £ s. d.

HOYLAKE MY 26 99

Handed in at Prestwick 3.42p Received here at [illegible]

TO Golf Club

Ball one up at 32nd hole playing splendidly

N.B.—This Form must accompany any inquiry made respecting this Telegram.

The telegrams from Prestwick

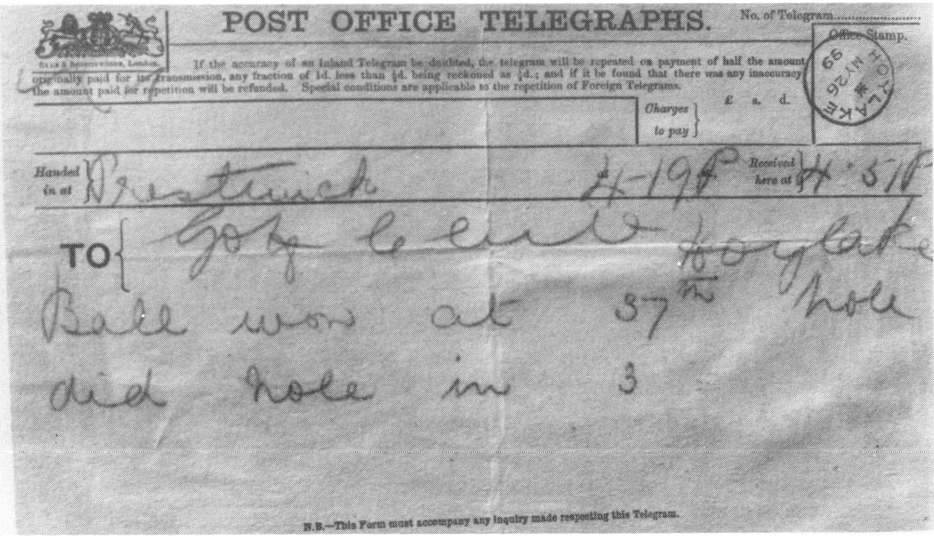

POST OFFICE TELEGRAPHS. No. of Telegram............ Office Stamp.

If the accuracy of an Inland Telegram be doubted, the telegram will be repeated on payment of half the amount originally paid for its transmission, any fraction of 1d. less than ½d. being reckoned as ½d.; and if it be found that there was any inaccuracy, the amount paid for repetition will be refunded. Special conditions are applicable to the repetition of Foreign Telegrams.

Charges to pay £ s. d.

HOYLAKE MY 26 99

Handed in at Prestwick 4-19P Received here at 4·51P

TO Golf Club Hoylake

Ball won at 37th hole

did hole in 3

N.B.—This Form must accompany any inquiry made respecting this Telegram.

and he was conveyed by human horses to the golf club for a further celebration.

A few weeks later, Leasowe, his other club, hosted a dinner for him at the Exchange Hotel in Liverpool. The captain, as chairman for the evening, spoke of the 'amiability and unselfishness of his character which endeared him to all'. Johnny, much overcome by the tributes, like Lord Kitchener in his aversion to speech making, made a short reply thanking his friends for the very hearty reception they had given him.

Tait and Ball at Ganton for the International Foursomes

9 — The Boer War (1899 - 1901)

If anyone had made the suggestion that next year's Championships would be played without the two great protagonists of Prestwick, it would have been greeted with disbelief.

For some time trouble had been brewing in South Africa. Cape Town was strategically vital to Britain in terms of communication with the eastern outposts of their empire, and the stability of the territory to the north of the Cape was therefore of great importance. This was also a time when the European powers were struggling for supremacy, and the Boers found themselves at the centre of the political posturing. On 9 October 1899 they declared war against Britain. Both Tait, an officer of the Black Watch and Ball as a volunteer with the Denbighshire Yeomanry, were shortly to embark for South Africa.

Before that however they had two further golfing encounters. In the late summer Vardon and Park were engaged in a challenge match over four greens, with Ganton as one of the venues. Johnny Ball and Freddie Tait joined them for a 36 hole foursomes exhibition the next day—another England versus Scotland trial of strength. The England pair were the better and won by 5 and 4.

At the beginning of October Freddie was in the vicinity of Blackpool and a further match between the two of them, over 36 holes at Lytham St Anne's, was arranged by the members. Lytham was almost a home club for Johnny. He had been a member there since 1893, was a regular visitor for their club competitions, and had won more than his share of the scratch medals. This time the happenings at Prestwick were reversed. Johnny outplayed the Scot over the first 18 holes and at one stage was four holes ahead. In the afternoon he was still 2 up coming from the 14th, but the 15th and 16th went to Tait. The 17th was halved, and so once again the result of the match rested on a single hole. Freddie bunkered his tee shot and Johnny was on for two. Another famous recovery shot from bunker to green followed and, as so often happens in matchplay, an unexpected thrust causes an opponent's mistake. Johnny three putted and the match was lost.

This as it turned out was Freddie's final game; within a fortnight he was preparing to embark for South Africa, spurred on at the thought of applying all his past training. His main worry was that the Boers would be defeated before he could reach the front. For no one expected the war to last more than a few months.

Meantime rumours were rife that Johnny intended to volunteer with the Denbighshire Yeomanry, the 29th Company of the Imperial Hussars. There was however some conjecture that he would be rejected by reason of his being over the age limit of 35.

Before his decision to go was made there was one further tribute to mark his success in winning the Championship for the fifth time. Shortly after the Prestwick victory, the Royal Liverpool council had set up a sub-committee to determine how it should be marked. A letter was sent to members inviting them to contribute to a commemoration fund, and over £300 was collected. With this it was decided that the Liverpool artist Mr R.E. Morrison should be commissioned to paint Johnny's portrait. Despite council's recommendation that he should be painted bare-headed, the familiar cap was painted in, Morrison over-ruling the council view. A further part of the fund went towards the clubhouse clock that still watches over the members as they make their way to the 1st tee. For Johnny himself there was a personal gift of a crested gold watch and chain. The St Andrews dinner was to be the occasion for these presentations, and a splendid one it was. The meal itself was a modest affair of a mere 11 courses. Following the Loyal Toast there were special toasts to 'The Amateur Champion', 'The Artist', not to mention 'St Andrews and Bonnie Scotland' and the 'Champion's Father' and the 'Club's Founder Members'. The captain spoke in a 'humorously eulogistic and happy manner' and Johnny responded 'in a more elaborate manner than is usually associated with the toasts to which he is called upon to respond ... though he is a man of deeds rather than words, his few words have usually the salt of humour about them.'

As to the painting, all were agreed that it was a good likeness, but there was some jocular comment about the Scottish element in the club which caused it, once presented, to be retained by the club to hang on the main staircase. Thank goodness for the Scottish element, as that is where the portrait still hangs today. The dinner ended with the singing of some specially composed verses in honour of the Champion and set to the music of 'Jack's the Boy'.

What were Johnny's motives in volunteering for South Africa? He was a fine horseman and an excellent shot, and he had a few years earlier been a member of the Wirral troop of the Earl of Chester's Yeomanry, attending annual camp with

John Ball by R. E. Morrison

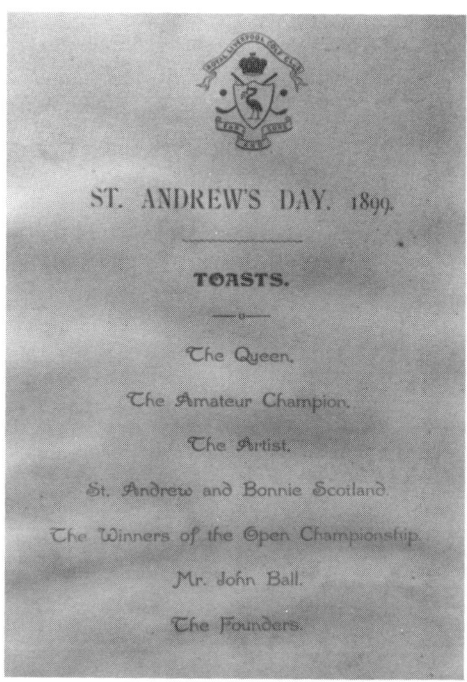

ST. ANDREW'S DAY. 1899.

TOASTS.

The Queen.

The Amateur Champion.

The Artist.

St. Andrew and Bonnie Scotland.

The Winners of the Open Championship.

Mr. John Ball.

The Founders.

them each year; but the troop was disbanded and Johnny had retired. Ted Salvidge of West Kirby had also been a member of the same troop, and when they disbanded he had transferred his allegiance to the Denbighshire Yeomanry. Ted, who was Harold Hilton's brother-in-law, was an all-round sportsman—a county rugby player, an athlete and swimmer. Despite the fact that he was nearly ten years younger than Johnny he was one of his closest friends, and it seems likely that it was Ted's influence that confirmed his decision.

THE IRISH GOLFER.
A WEEKLY RECORD OF THE ROYAL GAME.
Ireland's Only Golfing Journal.
VOL. I.—NO. 27. DUBLIN, FEBRUARY 21, 1900 TWO PENCE.

MR. JOHN BALL, JUNIOR.

PHOTO BY COOPER, BIRKENHEAD.
AMATEUR CHAMPION (1888, 1890, 1892, 1894, 1899).
IRISH CHAMPION (1893, 1894, 1899).
OPEN CHAMPION (1890).

John Ball on the charger

In December there were more rumours that he might be declared unfit by the medical board. Johnny himself was saying nothing and the press were unable to substantiate them. 'His view is the essentially unmodern one—whether he goes to Africa, or stays at home is a matter that concerns him first, the Boers secondly and the general public not at all.' It was however a matter for the friends in his various golf clubs, and, once it was established that he was to go, they subscribed for his charger. £15 were contributed by each of his three clubs — Lytham, Leasowe, and the Royal Liverpool. There were more gifts of a mauser pistol and some field glasses. By mid-January he was undergoing training initially at Wrexham and then in Aldershot. Details of his sailing to South Africa were finalised for early February. Before his departure he made one final visit to Hoylake, news of which was leaked and two hundred or so gathered at the station. He left 'with the engine exploding fog signals and the crowds cheering themselves hoarse'. In the press there were articles speaking of 'the happy association of sport with patriotism' and 'all honour to those who prefer the storming of the kopje to the bunker'.

Just after he had left, some tragic news broke. Freddie Tait had been wounded and hospitalised in December. By the end of January he had recovered and returned to the front. On the 7 February in a letter home he wrote 'The Boers seem to be in considerable force here, as they have attacked on the last three days. Today they are making a more determined attack, but have not attacked our position of the outpost line yet.' A few hours later they had and Freddie was dead, shot in the chest leading a charge to a position from which a counter attack could be made.

It is difficult to follow the movements of the Denbighshire Yeomanry and the actions of Trooper Ball over the next 18 months, but there were a number of letters from other local Yeomen, and a few press reports that made reference to Johnny. In July it was said that he had already seen much active service, but sadly he had to put up with the loss of his charger. In the autumn he was reported to have sustained an injury in a fall from his horse. This 'necessitated his having medical attendance for some slight hurts to one of his legs'. The doctor, a stranger, who attended the trooper, was evidently a golfer, as he immediately recognised his patient and exclaimed 'Why you are Johnny Ball the Champion golfer. I had the pleasure of seeing you play in the final against Freddie Tait at Prestwick.' This may have accounted for the fact that during his short period of recuperation he played his one game of golf in South Africa at Harrismith.

It was during the last two months of 1900 that the company were continually and heavily engaged. One act of heroism by Johnny was referred to in a letter home by Trooper Hinde from Rock Ferry:

> *I forgot to mention that Monday, being Bonfire night, we burnt two farms alongside which we encamped. In the gallop from the breakwater one man's horse came down, and John Ball immediately pulled up and went to his assistance, getting the horse up from the poor beggar's legs—all this of course under very heavy crossfire ... Ball is too modest to speak about himself in any such connection and won't have his name in the papers if he can possibly help it.*

The act was however reported in *Golf Illustrated* with the final comment: 'whether the deed will be considered sufficiently distinctive to gain the recognition of the authorities the future alone can decide — but his many friends, and they are legion, sincerely trust and hope that it will.'

A few weeks later a further letter from Ted Salvidge spoke of a miraculous escape for him. 'Ball lost his horse, and had to race on foot after his company for a long distance with the hidden Boers sending a shower of bullets up after him.' Sadly his friend was severely wounded a few days later and died before proper medical treatment could be obtained. This was clearly a great blow to Johnny and he described in a letter home to his sister the unhappy task of sorting through Ted's possessions and helping to dig the grave. The letter ended with the hope that he would soon see the end of the sad scenes he was forced to witness.

The next news was not until May of 1901 when again the Yeomen were involved in chasing the enemy on the Basutoland borders. Trooper Hinde, writing of a battle against a group of Boers who were found hiding near a farm, described how they occupied some kraals and for 40 minutes bullets were hailing around. He went on:

> *John Ball had a little Basuto pony of which he is very proud, and I saw him lying in the open with his reins over one arm blazing away for dear life. He told me afterwards several bullets passed between his arm and the horse, but he seemed more concerned*

about the beloved pony than his own safety. One bullet actually grazed his neck leaving a mark there.

More news came a few days later. The Denbighshire Yeomanry were returning home.

So, early in July Johnny arrived in Hoylake amidst scenes similar to those at the time of his departure. Indeed he might have been returning from yet another Championship victory. Five to six hundred people were there to greet him.

Laying him dead on the green

Mr Ball's train was sharp to time and amidst the explosion of fog signals and the shrill blast of the time horn of a factory adjacent to the railway station, Hoylake's hero—a bronzed, upright, khaki-clad figure came home. A great shout of welcome went up and Mr Ball's friends vied with each other in the heartiness of their greetings. When the handshakes had somewhat abated, Mr Ball, taking his sister's arm in his, led the way to the carriage which awaited him, followed by his Father. They had no sooner taken their seats than the horses were outspanned, and a body of Hoylake stalwarts seized the shaft and bore the party off at top speed to their home.

His home-coming however was a family affair and any ideas of festivities had been restrained by the sadness at a family bereavement a week earlier.

10 — Back on the Links (1901 - 1902)

Johnny was back on the links within a few days, and he seemed to have lost none of his skill. His driving was said to be as powerful as ever and his short game was all that could be desired. He did however remark of his clubs that 'they felt more like feathers in comparison with the more deadly weapons he had been accustomed to carry lately.' As so often happens after a long lay-off, subsequent games were not as easy as the first one, and his medal scores were a dozen or so shots more than would have been expected of him prior to his encounters with the Boers. By the autumn however he was in form again with wins at Lytham and Leasowe, including at the latter club the Captain's Cup, which he had won each time he had entered, thus inviting the remark by one of his friends: 'even if Johnny came home from the front with a wooden leg, he would still win the Captain's Cup.' Another Leasowe friend said that he wouldn't back himself to beat him even if he was playing with an umbrella. This followed a challenge in which Johnny received a third (6 shots) playing only with his putting iron, against the opponent, a scratch man, playing with his full set of clubs. He was round in 85, putting one shot dead from a bunker, and won his bet with ease. He ended the year with a remarkable round in the Boxing Day competion at Leasowe—a 68, the lowest competition score he ever achieved, which won him the handicap prize with seven shots added to his score.

Backswing and follow-through

The golfing scene had changed in a number of ways during his absence. Firstly the gulf between professional and amateur in terms of standard of play had widened dramatically. The three great players of the period, the Triumvirate, as they were dubbed by Horace Hutchinson, had now established themselves. Vardon had won his third Open Championship in 1899 and finished runner-up in the two subsequent years. J.H. Taylor won his third in 1900 and in 1901 Braid became Champion for the first time. Whilst the first prize for the Open was still just £50, there were now a number of other tournaments offering equivalent or better prize money. Meanwhile across the Atlantic the game was expanding so rapidly that there were more than a thousand listed golf clubs. This created the opportunity of great riches for the British professionals, both in terms of job opportunities and in tournaments and exhibitions. Prize money was far higher, and even appearance money was paid.

Without Tait and Ball, only Harold Hilton of the amateurs could begin to match the professionals. He had been a worthy winner of the Amateur crown both at Sandwich in 1900 and St Andrews in 1901, but no new names were emerging.

Articles on the ethos of amateurism were, however, filling the columns of the golfing magazines. Championship golf was an expensive business. A Hoylake player competing in the Amateur Championship at Sandwich would need to find a guinea for the entrance fee (the golf club's subscription at the time was just three guineas), 47 shillings and 6 pence for the return rail fare, and 35 shillings for accommodation and meals, 10 shillings for caddies, and another 10 shillings for golf balls (a shilling each). Allowing for other expenses, cabs and a few drinks, there would be little change from £8. Not much, the golfer of today might say, but with an inflation factor of about 5,000 per cent, it is the equivalent of £400 today. How then should the less wealthy amateur be given greater opportunity to compete? Or should the distinction between amateur and professional be abolished? It is clear that some of the top amateurs were benefiting financially from their skill.

> *A distinguished amateur at present is sought after by many people for the exploitation of their business—not because he is the best golfer, but because he is the best amateur. If the distinction were removed, he would at once find his proper market value and would not enjoy the inflated price he now commands. Hotel proprietors would no longer offer him free board and transportations, golf club makers would not hanker after his testimonials, nor editors clamour for his copy; temptation would be removed from his path.*

The greatest change of all was in equipment. Previously it was American golfers that imported British clubs, but now the reverse was happening as the socketed drivers became popular. As early as March 1899 there were reports of a new ball with a centre of rubber which was tightly wound round with gut and then with fine twine and coated with gutta-percha. Tests proved interesting. 'Those present made their drives with the standard ball, but the inventor of the new ball outdrove us all with a one handed shot with a putter.' The ball was to say the least a little lively; it had another fault: 'Not one of them has withstood more than four hits from a driver.' In the next two years these faults were being rectified, and by the autumn of 1901 the Haskell ball had arrived and Walter Travis, never renowned for his long hitting with the guttie, had won the US Amateur Championship using one of them. By November a few had reached this country. Hilton thought the claims that it could be hit 40 to 50 yards further were much exaggerated; 10 to 20 yards was nearer the length advantage and much of that was dissipated by the difficulty of controlling it for the short shots. Many of the professionals were also doubtful about its merits. The greatest barrier to its general use was the fact that it cost 2 shillings and 9 pence, for which amount one could get three good gutties.

Throughout the last few months of 1901 and the first of 1902 one other major topic absorbed the golf writers—the inauguration of an England versus Scotland international match. At the first Royal Liverpool council meeting of the year, Harold Janion the new secretary suggested that 'in consideration of what had appeared in the press, and of the impossibility of expecting any lead from the R & A, an international match be played at Hoylake on Saturday 26th April.' This was the weekend prior to the Amateur Championship which, together with the Open, was

The first international match — the England team. (Back row) B. Darwin, J. A. T. Bramston, H. C. Ellis, Hon. O. Scott, S. H. Fry, G. F. Smith and (seated) H. Hutchinson, J. Ball, H. Hilton and C. Hutchings

to be played at Hoylake that year. At the meeting a press release was approved giving the other proposed details—the match would be singles with two series of 18 hole matches. The side gaining the overall advantage in holes would be the winners. Hutchinson, Hilton and Hutchings for England and Laidlay, Low and Blyth for Scotland were to be the selectors. Royal Liverpool were congratulated from all quarters for their initiative, which implied some criticism of the Royal & Ancient who had turned down a similar proposal in 1898. The only points of controversy were the decision to score by holes rather than by matches, and the fact that John Graham spurned his English upbringing and opted to play for Scotland, his parents' birthplace.

Despite the fact that Hilton was the holder of the Amateur Championship, Ball was picked to play in the top single against Robert Maxwell of Scotland. Large crowds followed this game in which Johnny, playing with the Haskell ball, which he now favoured, took one hole off the Scot in the morning and halved in the afternoon. Hilton played Laidlay immediately behind and had some harsh words about the stewarding, and foreboding for the coming Championship.

Johnny driving in the match, watched by opponent Robert Maxwell

The spectators who followed Messrs Ball and Maxwell were quite a disorganised rabble and the men in charge of the rope were quite unable to keep them in check. Everyone seemed so anxious to obtain the best situations that they run and scramble. They do not seem to understand the bigger the circle made the better can everyone see. Another little matter which might be pointed out is the fact that it is not quite considered etiquette to break into unseemly mirth when a player misses a short putt. It may appeal to the spectators as ludicrous but it is rather a painful matter to the player who is surely worthy of a little consideration. Another disturbing element is the camera fiend. I had a little experience of one on Saturday last. Going to the first hole in the second round

I had actually addressed my ball and was considering the advisability of changing my club, when I felt someone touch me on the arm and on looking round gazed upon an apparition with a camera. I cannot repeat my reply to his request that I should stand still on swinging so that he could take a snap-shot, but I know I promptly hit my ball off the socket of the iron and put it into the field. After playing another ball I looked round for my aggressive friend, but he had melted away in the crowd.

Hilton lost his match, as did Horace Hutchinson to Graham, and the Scotland middle order proved stronger as well, so that the final outcome was victory to Scotland by seven holes.

As for the Amateur Championship that followed, by twist of fate Johnny and

Emerging from the clubhouse for the afternoon play

Robert Maxwell met again in the second round and this time the guttie outplayed the Haskell, with Maxwell taking the match at the 17th. Once again, however, Hoylake produced a home-bred winner, after an astonishing final. Charles Hutchings, a past captain of the club, who had only started golf at the age of 30 and was now 53, played Sydney Fry, a fellow member of the defeated English team. Hutchings had completed the first 18 holes in 75 shots and was 8 up, a position which he still held after six holes in the afternoon. With age beginning to tell and some splendid play by Fry, the Hoylake player had lost all but one of them as he came to the final green. On in two, he was left with two putts for the match:

Eight yards can look a very long way when at the end of the Championship two putts are required for victory. His first effort was a bad one—nothing like dead—but he holed the next amidst a mighty burst of cheering from the Hoylake supporters.

A month later the crowds were gathering again at Hoylake for the Open Cham-

INTERNATIONAL MATCH, 1902.

DINNER.

Hors d'Œuvres

Clear Turtle — Bonne femme

Soles — Tartar Sauce

Vol au vent à la Financière

Tournedos à la Provençale

Saddles of Mutton

Capons à la Bechamel

Tongue à la Ecarlate

Asparagus

Chartreuse of Apricots — Champagne Jellies

Mushrooms on Toast

Charles Hutchings

pionship. Johnny played with Sandy Herd for his first practice round, and as Herd recounts in his autobiography:

> *From that moment Mr Ball took as much interest in me as if we had been life-long friends. He was using the Haskell ball, and doing such wonders with it that I found myself envying him. I had not seen the rubber-cored ball before, and when we reached the 15th hole, Mr Ball smiling gave me a Haskell to try.*

It was love at first sight and when Herd returned to the club he went straight to Jack Morris's shop and purchased four of them, all that Jack could let him have.

After the first two rounds of the Championship, Herd with a 77 and a 76 was four shots behind Vardon. For the final day, by coincidence, he was paired with Johnny, who had had two 79s. This clearly suited Herd who in difficult conditions in the third round achieved a splendid 73:

> *I do not hesitate to say at this distance of years that Mr Ball was much more desirous that I should win than that he should beat me. He played his best, to be sure, but in many quiet ways — all within the Rules of course — he gave me every encouragement that one could give another.*

This was all the more necessary as the shots began to slip away in his final round of 81. Johnny was still alongside 'fully understanding my thoughts', as Vardon following close behind, and needing a 4 to tie, bounced the cross bunkers and came to within 20 yards of the pin. Three putts were to follow and Braid later, with a 3 to tie, could only manage a 4.

So it was that 1902 was the year of the H's—Hutchings, Herd, Hoylake and Haskell.

11 — Victory on the Old Course (1903 - 1907)

From the record books it might be assumed that Johnny's play over the next four years was following a natural pattern of decline. With his enforced break from competition, and now that he was over 40, there was certainly no reason to expect further success. He was however 'news'. At the championships and international matches, he, amongst all the amateurs, commanded the greatest press and public interest, and at times the quality of his play still justified this.

Follow-through with a mid-iron

A Royal Liverpool team led by Mr A.H. Crosfield MP who moved in high society, went to France in the spring of 1903 to play a match against the Grand Duke Michael of Russia's team. Crosfield's team included Ball, Hilton and Graham, and Harold Hilton writing of the former said: 'I can never remember him playing more brilliantly consistent golf than he did at Cannes ... Not only hitting the ball a long way, but in addition literally placing it where he likes.' Not too literally one hopes!

The Grand Duke brought a team back to Hoylake, and there was one unusual event after the main match had been played. Johnny partnered the Countess of Torby, the Duke's wife, in a friendly foursome against the Duke and Harold Hilton. 'Mr Ball I have seen in many circumstances', wrote John Low, 'bearing himself with credit and success, but never have I seen him play in a mixed foursome.' Perhaps this gave him the taste for it, for later that year, he was recorded as reaching the semi-final of the Moreton Ladies mixed foursomes playing with one of his sisters.

In his Championship appearances from 1903 to 1906 he was not so successful. He reached the fifth round once and was eliminated in the early rounds on each of the other occasions. The draw had not been kind to him. In 1905 at Prestwick he found himself playing his old adversary Laidlay in the first round with Robert Maxwell waiting for the winner. It was Laidlay who snatched that match from 1 down with four to play. Next year at Hoylake they met again in the third round, and despite Johnny's home advantage he lost again on the last green. He played only twice in the Open Championship during this period. The size of the entry now necessitated the elimination of those with the highest scores after the first two rounds, and though he did qualify for the second day on each occasion, he finished outside the top ten. It was Hoylake's John Graham who carried the amateur flag in those Championships finishing in seventh place in 1904 and fourth in 1906. Both times he was leading amateur and was only deprived of that honour in 1905 as well by the fact that his playing partner for the final round withdrew due to indisposition and Graham, the only amateur left in the field, pulled out with him. He had taken 85 in the third round to add to his first day score of 167.

The England *v* Scotland International matches continued as part of the Amateur Championship meeting and Johnny retained his position at the head of the England team with Robert Maxwell top for Scotland each time. Maxwell won three out of these four encounters. He always seemed to reserve his best play for Johnny. A morning round of 73 and out in 36 in the afternoon at Muirfield in 1903 gave him an 8 and 6 win. Next year he was 33 for the first nine holes at Sandwich, but on this occasion Johnny levelled the match and only lost as a result of two stymies on the three extra holes that were necessary — fuel for the stymie abolitionists who took another 40 years to win their way. He lost again in 1905, but back at Hoylake in 1906 there were only two England winners, and he was one of them, reversing the 1903 margin.

John Graham Junior

In July of 1905 John Ball senior, who had been unwell for some time, died. Latterly his main pleasure had come from sitting in his chair in the back parlour of the Royal Hotel recounting the doings of his famous son, and remembering some of the foursomes matches of the 1870s — the old cry 'Me and my son will play any two' — and his famous match for £100 with Davie Strath against Allan and Molesworth from Westward Ho! and a later occasion when the Right Honourable A.J. Balfour arrived unheralded at Hoylake and Johnny and Thosper were summoned to make the four. He was so much part of Hoylake's early history, and was a loved and respected character, as evidenced by the large number of locals that attended his funeral. For Johnny the Royal Hotel was never to be quite the same again.

Nothing happened in the early months of 1907 to foster hopes of further victories. In May, a preview of the Championship to be held at St Andrews reported on the Hoylake Spring Medal:

Mr John Graham in consequence of Mr Hilton's rejuvenation only won one medal, and John Ball was some strokes behind, but the latter is always a dangerous man in a Championship, if not the most dangerous, and the worse he has been playing before, the more likely he is to produce his best when it is wanted.

Even so the omens were not good. He had not previously mastered the subtleties of the Old Course, and whilst he did beat Robb, the previous year's Champion, in the international match the standard of play had been scrappy. The entry for the Championship was numerically the highest yet with more than 200 competing, and most incredible of all he was once again drawn to play Laidlay in the first round, their eighth contest in Amateur Championships. Hilton and Robb were also barring the way to the semi-final in that quarter.

As it turned out the match with Laidlay was the best of the Championship. Johnny reached the turn in 35 to Laidlay's 37 and was 2 up. Laidlay squared by the 13th, but Johnny restored his lead by the time he reached the Road hole. Here his drive found a deep cart rut and it looked certain that the match would go to the last hole, but he played a spectacular recovery shot, reached the green in 3 and won the match.

He continued to play well and only Bell of Westward Ho! extended him by taking him to the home green. The greatest talking point in the early rounds was young Gallaher, an R & A club waiter who had learnt his golf at County Down. He found himself matched against the Hon. Osmund Scott, an English international, in the second round, and gave the locals something to cheer with the waiter beating the Earl's son and showing scant respect for superior class. Meantime the other favourites were falling thick and fast. E.M. Byers, the United States Champion, was beaten in the second round. Hilton beat Robb the holder but then fell to Robert Andrew of Scotland. Maxwell lost to Feaver and Graham to Edward Blackwell. So in the quarter final on Friday morning, of the fancied players, only two of Scotland's winning team and Ball himself remained — all in the bottom half of the draw. By the afternoon Ball alone was left, he had beaten Andrew and now played Guy Campbell — the victor against Blackwell. It was Campbell who took an early lead, but Johnny recovered and the match was square with three holes to play. From the 16th tee both players drove over the railway onto the Madras playing fields — not out of bounds in 1907. From there Ball with his cleek played 'the shot of the Championship' as Harold Hilton described it, and one hole later he was through to his eighth final.

His opponent was a Midlander from Handsworth, C.A. Palmer aged 48, who had taken to golf late in life, and had a short and somewhat stiff swing. The odds were firmly in favour of the ex-Champion. A strong north-east wind blew and 'drenching rains swept over the course in sheets, pelting the players mercilessly and wrecking the umbrellas and otherwise adding to the discomfort of those watching the play'. Still there were 2,000 or so who who ventured out. The play was no better than the weather. Mental toughness counted for more than a smooth swing. Johnny held his game together better and despite injuring his wrist at the

Rough weather during the 1907 final at St Andrews

Ball and Palmer on the 4th green

Ball 2 up at lunch

third hole was 4 up after 13 holes. The rain and cold took their toll and his round ended with three 6s and two 7s. The lead was reduced to 2. Approximate scores were 90 for Ball and 92 for Palmer. The weather scarcely improved in the afternoon, but Johnny's powers of endurance and superior technique were too much for Palmer. Even with a 7 at the 4th hole his score was only a few over 4s and the match ended at the 14th. His main concern was a speedy return to the refuge of the clubhouse and to escape the ordeal of 'chairing'. He made a dash for it across the ladies' putting green and onto the sands, but his retreat was cut off and he ended up after all on the shoulders of his supporters in triumphant march across the 1st fairway. A few minutes later he was receiving the trophy and medal from the captain of the Royal and Ancient—none other than Leslie Balfour Melville, the man who had beaten him at the 19th in the final 12 years earlier.

Back at Hoylake the following day, a crowd of about 1,000 gathered at the station for the old routine—hooting, sirens, a brass band, cheering—and then the fishermen dragging the horseless carriage back to the club for further celebrations.

Once again the Royal Liverpool council decided that his victory should be marked in some way, and a further £100 was raised by subscription from members and went towards a replica of the cup he had won for the sixth time. Although, in his will, he left this trophy to the club, sadly it disappeared when the cups were dispersed to members' homes for safe keeping during the air raids of 1941, and has never reappeared.

The next honour came from a most unexpected quarter. At the autumn business meeting of the Royal and Ancient Golf Club it was announced that he was to become an honorary life member of the club, — 'normally reserved for Princes of blood or other distinguished persons — such distinction never accorded for purely golfing merit.' It was a mark of appreciation for the man as well as the golfer. *The Scotsman* applauded the R & A for doing this 'graceful thing' and went on to describe him as 'the same quiet genial and kindly man, more disposed to listen to an account of some other's game than to hear his own praises sung.'

Whether the committee of the R & A were aware that the Champion's golf shoes were on display in the window of A. Parry & Son, Shoemaker, 21/23 Moorfields, Liverpool, and that this fact was advertised in the local press, one does not know. Nor does one know whether he paid the full price for them, but anyway the concept of 'lending name and likeness' as a breach of amateurism had not yet arrived

GOLF *ILLUSTRATED.*

THE WEEKLY ORGAN OF THE "ROYAL & ANCIENT" GAME.

No 417. Vol. XXXII. FRIDAY, JUNE 7, 1907. Price Sixpence.

CHIEF CONTENTS.

	Page		Page
TEE SHOTS. Illustrated	201-3	*CORRESPONDENCE*	214
THE AMATEUR CHAMPIONSHIP. Illustrated.	205-10	*IRISH NOTES*	216
GOLF IN FOOZLEDOM. Written and Illustrated by HARRY FURNISS. Chapter VI.	211	*EVENTS OF THE WEEK*	217
WEST OF SCOTLAND NOTES	212	*COMPETITIONS*	218-22
GOLF QUERIES	213	*THE ACROSTIC*	224

1888.

Successfully employed in seven Championships.

✦ ✦ ✦

Has stood some 7,500 rounds.

✦ ✦ ✦

Warranted not to crack or lose form.

✦ ✦ ✦

Equally good in match or score play.

HOYLAKE
1890, 1894.

PRESTWICK
1888, 1890, 1899.

1907.

Combines length of drive with steadiness on the green.

✦ ✦ ✦

Most popular Ball with all golfers.

✦ ✦ ✦

CANNOT be obtained by the dozen.

✦ ✦ ✦

Unbeatable in all weathers.

SANDWICH
1892.

St. ANDREWS
1907.

The best ball

12 – The Mascot (1908 - 1910)

There were two new topics for the golfing press in the early part of 1908. The first was the Amateur Championship, with concern at the ever-increasing size of the entry, and the pressure to introduce a third English venue. A plan for strokeplay qualifying was canvassed by some, whilst others suggested that those that entered who could not play to a handicap of scratch should not be accepted— nothing much changes in golf. As to the extra venue, Deal and Westward Ho! were proposed as links worthy of inclusion on the rota. Others pressed strongly for an Irish alternative with Dollymount, now Royal Dublin, the favourite.

The other topic was the Olympic Games, which were to be held later that year. Golf had been on the list of Olympic sports in 1900 and 1904. On the last occasion at St Louis there had been 75 entries, all from the USA and Canada, and the gold medal had been won by George Lyon of Canada, who beat the United States Champion in the final. It appears that the R & A had been approached to join the British Olympic Council some two years earlier but there had been no reply, and so Mr Ryder Richardson, now secretary of Royal St George's was co-opted, and plans were made for the Olympic tournament to be held there, and at Deal and Princes—two rounds on each course. The views of most of the players were that the Olympic Games and golf had little in common. As Horace Hutchinson said 'If the Greeks had invented golf they would surely have awarded medals for the longest drives.' Even then motives of national prestige were beginning to pervade the true Olympic spirit. At any rate the English and Scottish 'cracks', Johnny included, indicated that they would have nothing to do with it. Despite this, arrangements

John Ball at Wallasey

went ahead, and George Lyon travelled to London to defend his title, only to discover that he was the only entrant. He was asked to accept the gold medal, but declined. Since then golf has not featured as an Olympic sport.

Johnny's golf over the next two years remained at the highest level. Although he suffered one of his few heavy defeats in the Amateur Championship of 1908 at Sandwich, losing by 6 and 5 to V.A. Pollock from the R & A, he showed fine form in club competitions winning scratch medals at Formby, Wallasey, Leasowe, Lytham and Blackpool, the latter with a 68 in the play-off, which equalled his lowest recorded medal score. Back at home he all but repeated his feat of 21 years earlier in winning the six scratch medals. Had he played in the Summer Meeting he might well have done it. As it was he won five. His winning scores in the two days of the Spring Meeting were 79 and 80. A 77 and 75 won him the Dowie Cup and Kennard Gold Medal in the autumn, to which he added the medal at the St Andrews meeting with another 80. An average of 78 in 1908 with the rubber-cored ball, albeit on a longer course, against a fraction over 80 in 1887 with the guttie seems to suggest that his play might not have been so strong, but with the vagaries of the Hoylake weather and the stronger competition it was another remarkable performance. His other achievement that year was to lead the amateurs in the Open Championship. His score of 311 was an average of four shots a round better than his two 82s of 1890, but still he was 20 shots away from James Braid, the runaway winner. This was perhaps a truer reflection of improving standards.

So to the next milestone, the Amateur Championship of 1910. The entry that year at Hoylake was down to 160, but all the leading players were there. The early part of the Championship was notable for one of the historic 19th holes. The two great golfing scribes Horace Hutchinson and Bernard Darwin were matched together, the former having socketed his second at the 18th to lose a one hole lead. At the 19th:

> *Mr Hutchinson hit a beauty down the course while Mr Darwin lay in one of the grassy hollows to the right, rather badly. From thence he played into the bunker short of the corner of the race course. Then Mr Hutchinson forgot all the sage advice he is wont to give — and as a rule acts on. He took his brassie instead of his cleek or iron, and put two balls running out of bounds — his fourth stroke was safe but wide. At this time he had played two more. It was then Mr Darwin's turn. He got out of the bunker clear of the course and then proceeded solemnly to play three balls out of bounds, after which he gave up the hole, having played six shots and presumably exhausted his stock of golf balls. 'How to Play the Nineteenth Hole at Hoylake' by Messrs Hutchinson and Darwin would be interesting reading.*

It had been a good Championship for the local players. Five had reached the last 16 and Hilton, Graham and Ball moved on to the quarter-final. Johnny's progress had not been without anxiety. In the fourth round he had to be at his very best to beat J.B. Pease, who had reached the turn in 36. Four consecutive 3s on the way home swung the match Johnny's way. In the next round, against another Hoylake player, F.W. Weaver, he needed three perfect pars to retain the one hole lead he had gained at the 15th. The following morning he 'As usual started badly losing the first three holes' against the Scottish international Harris. A lucky break at the 16th helped him to stay in the match, and after two good halves at the 17th and 18th, it was a characteristic brassie shot second at the 19th that earned him a 3 and the match. From then it was plain sailing. A 5 and 4 victory over Abe Mitchell took him to the final and next day his golf was brilliant. The report in *Golf Illustrated* described his play: 'Mr John Ball won his seventh Championship by the finest golf he has ever played and perhaps the finest golf that has ever been played in the Championship.' In the morning he was round in 73 which included two stymies, and it was not long before his opponent C.C. Aylmer was shaking hands and his supporters were cheering yet another victory. He had only to play nine holes in the afternoon.

Amongst those supporters was one little golfing girl aged about 12 whose game was already showing great promise. Johnny had taken her under his wing. Seventy-five years later in a letter to the golf club, she tells a story of that Championship:

> *Some of the Committee, Mr Janion who was Secretary and Mr Stoddart the Captain came over to our house and said to me — 'Johnny Ball wants you to follow him for every hole and shot during the Championship. You are he believes his mascot, and if he wins we will give you the largest box of chocolates that has ever been made.'*
> *'I did, he did, and they did!'*

She carried a red steward's flag each day so that she could stay close to him for every shot and she was still at his side, red flag and all, at the presentation.

This little girl was later to make her mark in ladies' golf as Mrs M.L. Clark. She still lives happily in Winchester with memories of one or two other stories of her early days at Hoylake and how her path crossed with her great hero. She tells of two occasions which illustrate his kindly nature.

Ball putting against Aylmer

The presentation

My brother and I had ended our match on the Royal green and in the exuberance of the moment started a wild game of hockey on the green with our putters and golf balls. A roar stopped us in our tracks, and to our horror one of the green keepers very large and with a scarlet face was coming out of the Royal Hotel with John Ball. As we stood there shocked, the damage we might have done to a sacred green dawned on us. However John Ball took charge, calmed the green keeper and said 'I can guarantee they'll never do that again.' He got over the fence onto the green and walked with us to our house and said 'Don't worry, no one will ever hear about this — who won by the way?' Memory can't supply the reply but does force me to say a small girl burst into tears!

As background to the other story I should explain that as an exception I was permitted to play the Links; the members knew of me, and I wallowed in the publicity. I played round after round by myself except when my brother's holidays gave me a partner. Shaping up for my second at the Dun, having had a good drive I saw that a group of members were walking from the Club for lunch at the Royal. They stopped to watch me. Here was a glorious opportunity to show them—I took a tremendous swipe, caught the top of my brassie in my coat and let out a fearful oath (learnt from our keeper in Scotland). Peals of laughter came from the members but trouble was to follow. My father sent for me that evening, and the Links were forbidden for two days. 'But for your friend John Ball,' he added ' it would have been for a week.'

Whilst young Peg was enjoying her box of chocolates, the council of Royal Liverpool were looking for some new way to mark yet another Championship victory. He became the recipient of an honorary starting time for all club competitions, as the minutes of the council meeting dated 7 June 1910 reveal: 'The Captain proposed a hearty vote of congratulations to Mr John Ball on his winning the Championship for the seventh time and that he should have the privilege of being the first member to start on all Ballot days after the Captain, thc Hon. Treasurer and the Chairman of the Green Com-mittee. This was carried unan-imously.' At the next meeting an offer by one of the members, Mr A. Sinclair, to present a cup to celebrate the victory was also accepted, and this became the scratch prize for the Queen Victoria Commemoration Meeting, strangely, one of the few trophies on which the name of John Ball does not appear.

Johnny confirmed his position as the best amateur player of that year, by also finishing leading amateur in the Open Championship at St Andrews, as he had done at Prestwick two years earlier. It was not his score of 314 that was remarkable, but the fact that he had made the journey to St Andrews on a motor cycle.

"ZODIAC WINS"

1910

AMATEUR CHAMPIONSHIP

AT HOYLAKE.

WE HAVE THE HONOUR TO ANNOUNCE THAT

The WINNER of the CHAMPIONSHIP

PLAYED WITH A "ZODIAC"

ALSO

The "ZODIAC" was played by the FINALISTS.

2/- and an old "Zodiac" purchases a new **"ZODIAC."**

MARTINS-BIRMINGHAM, Ltd., Golf Ball Makers, BIRMINGHAM.

A cartoon after Ball's seventh victory

13 — Westward Ho! (1912 - 1914)

Next year, for a change, a different item appeared on the council agenda at Hoylake. It was how to mark the victories of Harold Hilton. He had not only won the Amateur Championship at Prestwick, where Johnny succumbed in the fourth round, but also the United States Amateur Championship at Apawamis near New York. To add to that he finished one stroke away from a play-off with Vardon and Massy in the Open Championship at Sandwich. As a result the Royal Liverpool members were once again asked to dig in to their pockets for a presentation. £140 was raised and it was agreed that a portrait should be painted to hang alongside that of Johnny's on the main staircase to the Clubroom.

The discussions amongst the clubs that ran the Amateur Championship had finally found in favour of Westward Ho! as the additional English venue. This had been chosen for the 1912 Championship. One of the natural consequences of picking a less accessible venue was a smaller entry — down to 140. The format for the international match between England and Scotland, played on the Saturday before the Championship, had also been changed. It was to be decided by five 36 hole foursomes matches. Despite the fact that there were only 15 Scots from whom their team had to be picked, they won again, by three matches to two. Johnny played with Abe Mitchell and lost to Robert Harris and Norman Hunter.

Robert Maxwell

This was the last of the series of matches that had started in 1902. Johnny had played each time and had led the England team in all the singles, but he had won only five of those ten matches, all his defeats being at the hand of Robert Maxwell. The heaviest was in 1909 when Maxwell on his home course, Muirfield, had played the first round in 75 to be 4 up, and then proceeded to do the first eight holes of the second round in 3, 4, 3, 3, 5, 4, 3, 4 winning seven of them. There were no excuses, no complaints. Johnny returned to the clubhouse looking thoroughly pleased with himself and told his sympathetic friends: 'I played damn good golf, otherwise I'd have been beaten by much more.'

Johnny on the 1st tee at Westward Ho!

It is not clear why the international matches were discontinued. Certainly the foursome format was not popular, and, with the large entry for the Amateur Championship, it was felt that it added unnecessarily to the physical demands of the week for the top players.

Back to 1912 and Westward Ho! It was in the international match that Robert Harris said jokingly to Ball, who was playing poorly: 'You're a lucky man. I have just heard that the Committee is going to make a rule that no one over fifty is to be allowed to enter the Championship.' He believed that Johnny was 49 and knew that he was becoming weary of it all. Johnny replied 'I wish they'd done this before and made the age limit 48. I didn't want to come here and play again.' But he had been overridden by his fellow club members of whom half-a-dozen had made the trip.

Once the Championship started Johnny's play began to improve and with a bye to the second round and four games, none of which went beyond the 16th, he found himself matched in the quarter-final against a local, F.S. Bond, who had no previous successful run in the Championship. Ball was therefore expected to win, but it was Bond who forged ahead and was 5 up with seven to play. Johnny was not, however, surrendering without a fight, and he pulled back two holes quickly. Still he was 3 down with three to play. With the honour at the short 16th he hit a brilliant shot to within a few feet of the pin, and his opponent followed into the bunker. Suddenly doubts gathered in Bond's mind and the possibility that he might lose began to dawn on him. With three more faultless holes from Ball, another miraculous escape had been effected. After this he had little problem in beating Hambro of Royal St George's in the semi-final, and was thus left to play Abe Mitchell from Cantelupe, the Ashdown Forest artisan club.

Johnny knew Mitchell's game from first hand. He had played with him not just in the international match, but in the semi-final of the Championship at Hoylake two years earlier. He was young and strong—and much longer than Johnny—but was prone to occasional wildness. Two other factors may have influenced the result—firstly the weather took a turn for the worse, and wet and windy weather had never hampered Johnny's chances. The second factor was that a body of locals from Bideford who knew little about golf had joined the crowd and as Bernard Darwin recounted:

> *They appeared to be imbued with a violent and wholly inappropriate 'class' feeling; there was a working man in the final and they had come to see him win. Not content with this reasonable partisanship they fanned themselves into a still warmer flame by imagining Mr Ball as the typical capitalist trampling on the honest workman. Their behaviour was at once venomous and absurd. It was utterly repugnant to Mr Mitchell, whom they supported, and did him no good and probably a great deal of harm. As for Mr Ball, if it had any effect on him at all, it was to harden his resolution and make him set his teeth even more tightly. To make him angry is the way to make him win.*

One incident at the 14th hole might have softened their attitude. Mitchell's tee shot to this short hole seemed to be heading for the edge of the green, but it landed on a spectator's open umbrella and shot at right-angles into a bunker. Johnny, reflecting the spirit in which he played, immediately said to Mitchell: 'Wash that one out and drive another ball.' Mitchell however, 2 up at the time, politely rejected the offer, accepting the mishap as a rub of the green, and by the end of the first round had increased his lead to three.

Memories of the Prestwick final against Tait, when he was 3 down at the half-way stage will have comforted him. The cause was by no means lost, particularly if he could hold his man over the first three holes against the wind where the extra length would be expected to tell against him.

Abe Mitchell

> *In fact Mr Ball did better than that, for he got one back; he had the turn of luck at the short hole and was now not only within striking distance but right on his enemy's heels. That enemy, however, had plenty of fight left in him, and the match went on with thrilling ups and downs till it was all square with three to play. On the sixteenth green Mr Ball with a putt for a half was laid what looked the deadest stymie that ever was laid, the adversary's ball on the brink of the hole and no apparent way round—no, not a ghost of a one. Mr Ball looked at his opponent with a smile, half quizzical, wholly good natured, and there are not many people who could smile at such a moment. Then he settled down to his putt and, with an aluminium putter of all unlikely clubs, played the shot at exactly*

the dead strength and by some miracle holed it.

All square with two to play, and then Mr Ball missed his second to the long seventeenth and Mr Mitchell was dormy. Both of them were over the black and oozy burn in two, neither was quite dead in three. I imagine each ball lay four or perhaps five feet away. Mr Mitchell had to play. This for the Championship! No doubt the putt looked horribly long to him at that moment. He pushed the ball out to the right of the hole, and made a gesture of stifled despair. Mr Ball rapped his in, right at the back of the hole, and the crowd rushed out across the burn again. The nineteenth was marked by two splendid recovery shots, Mr Ball from a bunker on the right, Mr Mitchell from a watery ditch on the left (it was the Alps at Prestwick over again), and the hole was halved in five. At this point I raced away down the fairway of the second hole in order to see the second shots. One ball came right down the middle of the course: that was Mr Ball's. There followed a long pause: no second ball came. What on earth had happened? Clearly some tragedy had overtaken Mr Mitchell, but what could it be? 'The match is over' — the word passed along and we rushed back bewildered. Mr Mitchell had topped his ball into a ditch and in trying to get out had hit the ball on to himself. Mr Ball had won his eighth championship. Will any man ever win so many again?

This was written some 15 years later — otherwise it might have been presumptuous to suggest that a ninth title was out of his reach. In the event he played in the last two Championships prior to the outbreak of the war in August 1914. At St Andrews in 1913, where Hilton achieved his fourth victory, he lost narrowly in the first round, and the following year at Royal St George's he reached the third round.

As a post-script to his Westward Ho! Championship victory the story is told by Guy Farrar that his Hoylake friends and admirers had gathered as usual at Hoylake station to do the honours on his return. But Johnny had had enough; he wanted no more fuss. 'The train steamed in, the fog signals went off, the crowd cheered, but the Amateur Champion was not there—he had left the train at the previous station and walked home along the shore!'

14 — The Post-War Years (1920 - 1940)

When competitive golf resumed after the Great War, the Hoylake domination of the amateur game was at an end. Hilton was over 50 and Ball nearer 60. Saddest of all, John Graham had been killed in action, and for all his great talent, he must simply be remembered as the finest amateur golfer never to have won the Championship. Whilst British golf lay dormant for six years, in America there was only a short disruption. It is not surprising therefore that they were now capitalising on the boost that had been given to the game by Francis Ouimet's famous victory against Vardon and Ray in 1913. The extent of this became evident in 1921, not just with four Americans in the top ten of the Open Championship, but from the inaugural amateur match between Great Britain and the United States which preceded the Amateur Championship at Hoylake. That was a black day for British golf. How

they could have done with the skills of Ball, Hilton and Graham at their best.

When the Championship started it was as if the clock had been turned back. Johnny once again was slipping unobtrusively through the early rounds. Three comfortable victories brought him up against J.H. Douglas junior, one of the victorious American team, in the fourth round. The evening before he had suggested: 'If only the wind and rain would sweep across the Dee from the Welsh hills, I think I could win.' In the event it was another day of sultry heat. Even so the large gathering of supporters saw one more famous victory, and those that didn't see it

Lygan-y-Wern

heard a great cheer go up as he holed for a 4 at the 19th. Age took its toll, and he fell in the afternoon to another member of the American team, F. Wright.

This was the Championship in which Bobby Jones made his British debut, losing in the fourth round to Allan Graham, or more truthfully losing to Graham's 'brazen serpent of a putter'. Allan went on to the final, a thing which his illustrious brother had never achieved but, with a heavy heart at the sad news that his father had died during the night, the match ended quickly and quietly.

Johnny was now living in North Wales. Before the war Lygan-y-Wern, a large white house set at the foot of the Halkyn hills near Holywell, had been owned by Oscar Smith, his brother-in-law. From his visits there, to stay with his sister and family, including young Lawrence, he came to love the place. In 1920 his name appeared on the electoral role as co-owner with Oscar Smith. Lawrence, then a teenager, remembers his uncle as a man who was more at ease out of doors with a golf club, a gun, or some garden implement, than in the house with book or pen.

The view over the Dee Estuary meant that with his binoculars he could still keep an eye on the links and the Royal Hotel, which were only an hour away on his motor cycle, and there was still a bed for him at the Royal Hotel whenever he wanted. The tranquillity of North Wales appealed to him. Behind the house there was some woodland, where the Halkyn hares suffered a similar fate to the Hoylake rabbits, and in a large paddock he could ease his stiffening joints with a few mashie shots under the watchful eye of his beloved donkeys. Their braying could be heard all over the district and the local children used to make special expeditions to feed Johnny Ball's donkeys. A few miles up the road on the hills above Holywell was the pleasant moorland golf course with an abundance of gorse and bracken. From time

John Ball and Oggie (alias 'Old Bill')

to time he played there. The story is told of his first visit, when he signed the visitors' book as J. Smith to avoid any fuss, and went off to the first tee. He was of course recognised and his money refunded. On another occasion a few years later he played there with Harry Vardon, both the names appearing in the visitors' book, Ball with his green fee of half-a-crown paid and Vardon with the words 'Professional golfer no fee'.

He still made regular visits to Hoylake, normally coinciding with club medals or matches. Until 1924 his name continued to appear amongst the medal winners, and he was still selected to lead the club in team matches against the Oxford and Cambridge Golfing Society, the Army Golfing Society, Sunningdale and the like.

Johnny during the 1924 championship

Oggie Jones his caddie would be waiting for him as he appeared, walking across the links from the Royal Hotel. Oggie was, to say the least, a little backward, and Johnny was in no need of advice. He would nominate a club for the ears of his opponent, and without waiting for Oggie to pick it out, would select some other weapon more appropriate for the job. On another occasion it is recorded that Oggie was caddying in a thick fog. 'Give me the putter and driver', his master requested after the second shot to the 17th had been played towards the green, 'and wait there and listen for the drive landing at the 18th.' Neither Oggie nor the clubs were seen again that day.

There are still a few more Championship appearances to record. In the Open of 1924 he could only manage an 85 at Hoylake, and the same at Formby, the other qualifying course, which was not nearly good enough to earn a place amongst the Championship qualifers. In 1925, the first English Championship was held at Hoylake and he played in that, reaching the third round. Two years later the Amateur was again at Hoylake. Ball and Hilton entered, and remarkably both of them were trying to win their hundredth Championship match. Johnny had a bye to the second round where he was to play another Hoylake member, J.R. Abercrombie. Hilton meanwhile had lost to Norman Sutton of the West Cheshire Artisans, later to make his mark in professional golf. The evening before his game Johnny had expressed anxiety about his driving—if he could get them away, he might win. 'The day came' as Bernard Darwin was to write:

And he drove beautifully, swinging his club with the grace and dash of youth, but the short putts—at least four of them, and two of them very short ones—beat him. As to the rest of his game it came infinitely nearer to perfection than that of almost all other golfers, forty years younger than him, who played that day. Once or twice, when the wind was blowing hard on his back and he had to try to gain distance, he was inclined to smother the shot; otherwise every ball was hit cleanly and truly from the exact middle of the club face.

One shot I shall never forget. I had gone out especially to see it played, namely the tee shot to the fourth hole, the Cop. The wind was that typical wind which makes the hole most difficult, sweeping across from right to left, so that ordinary mortals either hook far over the green or else hold the ball up too much and are bunkered on the right. Only the night before some of us had been talking about the shot, and a friend of Mr Ball's had quoted his oracular pronouncement as to how it should be played 'Well you hook it and slice it.' The moment arrived and the wind was blowing so freshly that most people thought Mr Ball would have to take a wood to it. He took his cleek, however, and hit the ball straight through the wind as if the wind did not exist. It finished eight or nine yards away straight past the pin, and then alas, he took three putts. Still our eyes had once more seen that shot played in the grand manner.

It was a great moment too, when Mr Abercrombie became dormie five, and Mr Ball began to fight with his back against the wall. Two great shots gave him a putt for 3 at the Field (490 yards or so and at 64 years old) and one hole came back. His enemy made a mess of the Lake against the wind and the second hole came back. The years seemed to have rolled away. Here was the irresistible spurt once again. Once again we were to see the impossible achieved. To the Dun Mr Ball played two fine shots and was unkindly caught in the little bunker that comes jutting out on the left. Still he got out; it seemed almost certain that he would have a putt to keep the match alive, and surely surely he would hole it. But all our beautiful dreams were destroyed by Mr Abercrombie holing a long putt in the odd. And so the hero went down glorious in defeat.

So, 49 years after his first appearance as a mere boy in the Open Championship of 1878 at Prestwick, he finally bowed out of Championship golf.

There is not much more to tell, although one further honour did come his way. In 1928 the Honourable Company of Edinburgh golfers, no doubt at the instigation of his old rival Robert Maxwell, invited him to become an honorary life member. This meant that he was a life member of seven clubs. As well as Royal Liverpool and the Royal and Ancient, Leasowe in 1900, Wallasey and Formby in 1907 and Royal Lytham and St Anne's in 1908 had all honoured him similarly. It would have been eight, but by then the Blackpool Golf Club no longer existed.

He had also been asked to become the first president of the Hittite Golfing Society formed in 1926. The fact that he declined was no surprise, as such positions were not to his taste. He did, however, present the society with a putter which is the much coveted trophy played for each year at the Hittite's Autumn Meeting.

A few years earlier Oscar Smith and his family had moved on from Lygan-y-Wern, and Johnny lived there with his unmarried sister Elizabeth and the housekeeper, Nellie Williams. Nellie was a strong character and her influence within the household and a growing relationship with Johnny created friction with the sister. When in July 1932 Johnny and Nellie, then aged 42, married at Holywell Registry Office the ill-feeling was such that all family affinity faded. When Johnny drew up his will the following year, other than some small bequests, one to Muriel Robinson, manageress of the Royal Hotel, and another, leaving his 1890 Championship medals to the Royal Liverpool Golf Club, Nellie was to become the sole beneficiary. None of the Ball or Smith family were mentioned, only poor 'Bessie'. 'If my wife shall predecease me and my old donkey Bessie shall be still living I direct the company to have my said donkey destroyed painlessly by a duly qualified vetinerary surgeon.'

His visits to Hoylake thereafter were few and far between. Some of the club's senior members recall a kindly old man walking the links and offering advice and encouragement. One remembers an occasion when as a junior he was setting out by himself from the 1st tee, and a caddy walked over to him and said 'Mr Ball asks if he might join you for a few holes?' The young John Graham, son of Allan, and nephew of John, as a boy played a round with the great man and recounts how he stood on the tee at the Cop hole, with its fearsome cross-bunker guarding the green, uncertain as to what club he should play. Could he make the carry with an iron, or was it a wood? The maestro's advice was to find the oldest ball in his bag, and hit it with his spoon.

When Championships were on, Johnny would be there to watch, to re-live his triumphs and to meet and talk with old friends. Golf, he felt, was becoming too easy — raked bunkers no longer made one scratch one's head, and the well-manicured greens were 'damned croquet lawns'. He was still a good judge of golfing ability and not averse to the occasional wager. 'I don't reckon him', he would observe, and a few bob would go on the other man.

With the dark days of 1939 and 1940 there was little left for him, and he died a few weeks before his 79th birthday in December 1940.

15 — In Perspective

Where does Ball stand in the history of the game? The story of his successes in the national championships and major competitions has been told. His achievements at club level, tabulated in the Appendix, were prolific — 168 Scratch Medals. Has any other golfer won so many?

To compare golfers of different generations is neither practicable nor productive; one may wonder how Bobby Jones would have fared with the guttie and half-a-dozen hickory-shafted clubs dressed in a tightly buttoned tweed jacket and starched collar, just as one may wonder whether Johnny would have enjoyed the metal-headed, graphite-shafted driver, and the lightning fast switchback greens of America? The answer, one can assume, is that in both cases they would have managed without too much trouble. The ability to adapt is one of the tests of greatness, and Johnny certainly demonstrated that.

Address and backswing

The follow-through

It is possible to make comparisons amongst golfers of the same generation, although, as most selectors know, even that is a difficult task. So—how did he rate with his contemporaries? Such was the length of Johnny's career that it stretches for 50 years from the age of young Tom Morris to that of Bobby Jones, two undisputed champions of the game. He watched the former at Hoylake in the 1870s and competed with the latter in the 1921 Amateur Championship. From the mid-1890s to the Great War the triumvirate—Vardon, Taylor and Braid—dominated the professional game and by then the amateurs were on a plane below.

Johnny was asked by his great rival Horace Hutchinson, who was writing one of his magazine articles in 1907, to say when he thought he was playing at his best. 'At the age of 14', Johnny responded. When challenged he admitted that perhaps his game had continued to improve until he was 16, but 'I was certainly playing better at fourteen than I am now'. Bernard Darwin admits that he 'never saw the real and most terrible Johnny Ball'. Whatever Johnny may have thought himself, results suggest that he was at his best during the period from 1887 to 1892, and bearing in mind that this was a period when no single professional was predominant, he could lay claim to be *primus inter pares* at that time. That is a prejudiced view and doubtless many would argue otherwise, but even today's sophisticated computer systems that are programmed to sort out the rankings of the world's top players have their critics! What can be said is that Johnny during that period, in terms of long straight driving and the ability to flight cleek shots into the greens, opened the eyes of the next golfing generation by setting new standards.

His success was based on the twin towers of temperament and technique. As for the former his modest demeanour and his quiet sportsmanship belied the self confidence and steely determination. No stories unfold of petulance or ungentlemanly conduct, though maybe, if the occasion demanded, he was not averse to a little gamesmanship. That was the exception however. More often he was a generous opponent, as displayed in one Championship when he was due to play

Bunker play with a mid-iron

an older golfer of no great ability in the first round. Johnny did not know him, but knew his wife, whom he met on the way back to the hotel in the evening. He politely remarked on his game next day with her husband. She told him that she doubted if he would play, as he was so terrified. Johnny then said: 'Would you please give him my compliments and say that, unless he is ill, I shall be most disappointed if he does not turn up.' The man duly turned up shaking with nerves. Ball won at the 18th green and no one could understand why so many apparently perfect shots finished in bunkers!

The elements of his technique were an old-fashioned palm grip, with his right hand underneath the shaft, learnt no doubt from the Scottish professionals who had visited Hoylake in his formative years, a wide and open stance, which in his later years became rather less wide and less open, and that 'wonderful well oiled turn of the body' swinging the club back to a position a little beyond the horizontal, then the free unhurried uncoiling of the shoulders and drive with the legs flowing into a graceful high follow-through. No one appreciated the sight of his swing more than Bernard Darwin. 'In that very poetry of movement, in that intangible quality called rhythm his style has never been excelled, and in the eyes of his worshippers can never be approached.'

He was a great exponent of the low-flying half shot — the pushed cleek. He would stand with body forward and feet close together, playing it with arms and wrists only. Nor did he find much difficulty in flighting the full shots low, when the weather required it. 'I happened to be driving a ball of just the right height for the day' he would say as he mastered the links at Hoylake once more in a gale force wind. As for his pitching, once again the cleek or mid-iron were the clubs he liked to use. These would suffice even from the deepest bunker. He never came to terms with 'the damned spade' as he would call the sand wedge, though it is said that he did once consent to play a bunker shot with one, and to his embarrassment holed the shot.

Had his putting matched the rest of his game 'Heaven knows', in the words of Darwin, 'how many Championships he would have won, and how few would have fallen to anyone else' but he always hated short putts. His fallibility no doubt could be attributed to being put to the test more often than most through aggressive approach putting. He certainly holed his share of longer ones. He constantly changed his putter, and it is said that in the 1899 Championship final his caddie offered a sheath of clubs on each green for his master to choose from — goose-necked putter or iron or driving cleek — they all did their share.

Whatever the view of the golfing pundits may be, for the locals in his native Hoylake it was a case of hero worship. 'The fall of a hero at Hoylake' was the headline for a feature article by Harry Beswick in *The Despatch* of 5 June 1906. Beswick, no golfer himself, arrived in time to mingle with the gallery who were returning to the club after watching Johnny's narrow second round victory in the Championship. 'Johnny who?' he had asked.

It wasn't until the afternoon that I awoke to the enormity of my offence. Johnny Ball it appears is the emperor of Hoylake, the lord of its fowl and its brute. He is also its golfing Pope, Chief Magistrate, Verger, Chancellor of the Exchequer, Archdeacon, Coroner, Presiding Barrister, Groom of the Backstairs, and Lord High Everything Else.

Incidentally he is the most popular man in the district. For a man to ask in Hoylake who is Johnny Ball is to court instantaneous death as a supposed criminal lunatic, or obtain an altogether false and erroneous reputation as a humourist. Hoylake people live but to bask in the light of Johnny's flashing cleek. Strong men bend the knee and salaam when he passes, and beautious maidens strew his path with roses and contend for the honour of kissing the hem of his club case.

Popular golfers are always accompanied round the course by admiring devotees. I joined the gallery which followed the admirable Johnny and with them tripped over the slippery turf, stormed stargrassed kopjes, and fell into diverse bunkers. We were a mixed company; gentle and simple, rich and poor, experts and duffers, men and women and children.

Mr Ball's opponent was also a great player, but, as a small boy put it to me, 'Norrinit with Johnny'. But the opponent had no respect for local prejudices. He was a person lacking a sense of proportion and perspective. The way that man scorned the dramatic unities was heartbreaking. He had the effrontery to win four holes from Johnny early in the round. Small boys holding on to the rope —which is carried by stalwart fishermen, so as to form a movable barrier—wept audibly. When the great man topped his drive, got into a bunker and found another in chopping it out, I felt alarmed for the health statistics of Hoylake, and had a desperate scheme for bringing up the Medical Officer of Health. 'Ah','Oh','Ooh?' groaned the gallery in piteous fashion. There were gathering tears and tremblings of distress; blanched cheeks and choking sighs— 'Johnny, Johnny, what are you doing?'

When, however, the opponent got into a bunker, the smile of the gallery was beautiful to behold. When the great man made the game all square the small boys, strung on the rope like cherries on a string, punched each other with the mutual affection of youthful hearts, with but one constant thought. As for the ladies they beamed and helped themselves to chocolates. As the game got to its final stage smaller crowds which had remained en potence on the small hillocks, joined the gallery. There was real excitement in the air. Ball one down and two to go. Will he square it?

He didn't and Beswick wisely melted away from the scene of gloom and despondency.

Why was Johnny the subject of such adulation, why did the crowds and the blue-jerseyed fishermen with their ropes follow him, cheering his victories, and leave the Hiltons and Grahams to play in comparative isolation? Why in the 1960s was it Arnie's army and not Jack's? There is nothing rational about hero worship. Maybe it was the fact that Johnny was the first of the locals to bring honours to Hoylake, or maybe they liked the strong, silent, undemonstrative type in an age when conformity, and fortitude were qualities to be admired. Whatever the reason, in the words of Guy Farrar: 'No-one has ever inspired greater hero worship — and no-one ever courted it less.'

Epilogue

The silhouettes of the houses at the end of Stanley Road can barely be identified as I sit at my desk, overlooking Hoylake's second fairway. To the left is the faint outline of the sand dunes, and nothing beyond—Hilbre Island, the pale glint of the estuary, and the Welsh hills have vanished. Soon the swirling fog will hide the flag at the 14th.

How dense, I wonder, was the fog when Johnny took his famous wager to complete his round in less than two and a quarter hours, in under 90 shots and without losing a ball. That was St Andrew's Day 1907. He duly won his bet using the same black ball for his 81 shots and with time to spare, but fortune favours the brave, for as he came to the 12th hole a hazy sun forced its way through the fog and the round was completed in perfect visibility.

There is an old Hoylake superstition that, if the body of a drowned seaman is washed ashore, and is not given a Christian burial, then he will remain to haunt the area. Such was the local explanation for a ghost at the Royal Hotel. A few years before the hotel finally closed, several staff members reported that they had seen a man dressed in a brown Norfolk jacket, knickerbockers and a tweed cap walking along the corridor from the hall to the ballroom, and then inexplicably disappearing. Was it a seaman? Or did he walk with head bowed, leaning forward, and was he wearing red socks? Who is this figure appearing through the murk, club in hand, striding purposefully towards the fence below me and on towards the spot where the old Stanley green used to be. Could it be Johnny, reliving his bet?

If I hurry downstairs I could catch him for a word or two. There are so many questions I would like to ask, so many gaps in this book to be filled. What about your schooldays? You went at first to the local school down King's Gap and were taught by Mr Turpin, but did you later go to boarding school? Your father played golf with young Tom, the Champion. Did his cousin Jack ever suggest that, one evening, he should play a few holes with Hoylake's infant prodigy? So many of your great golfing moments occurred at Prestwick. Was this your favourite links, and what were your feelings as you came to the 18th tee with the Open Championship in your grasp? The Old Course had less happy memories for you. Why did you select that pitching mashie for the final fateful shot over the burn at the 19th hole? Was it Freddie Tait or Ted Salvidge who encouraged you to enlist for the Boer War, and did you need to stretch the truth about your age to gain acceptance? You had a reputation for fallibility on short putts in your early days, yet in your final Championship wins this part of your game was more a strength than a weakness — what changed? Some new technique, a different attitude, another putter? Why did you move from Hoylake to North Wales, and what caused the rift between your sisters and Nellie? Whatever happened to all those medals?

No, it is not Johnny; it is one of the Hoylake Villagers searching for balls. The questions will have to remain unanswered; nor will there be the opportunity to apologise to him for my intrusion on his privacy.

The view from the author's desk

Appendix

I Ball's Open Championship Record

Year	*Venue*	*Score*	*Place*	*Winner*		*Leading amateur*	
1878	Prestwick	165	5th	Jamie Anderson	157	Ball	165
1879	St Andrews	Did not play		Jamie Anderson	169	Smith	180
1880	Musselburgh	Did not play		Bob Ferguson	162	—	
1881	Prestwick	Did not play		Bob Ferguson	170	—	
1882	St Andrews	Did not play		Bob Ferguson	171	Boothby	175
1883	Musselburgh	Did not play		Willie Fernie	159	Rolland	167
1884	Prestwick	Did not play		Jack Simpson	160	Doleman	178
1885	St Andrews	No return		Bob Martin	171	Hutchinson	178
1886	Musselburgh	Did not play		David Brown	157	Laidlay	162
1887	Prestwick	Did not play		Willie Park Jnr	161	Laidlay	166
1888	St Andrews	Did not play		Jack Burns	171	Balfour	175
1889	Musselburgh	Did not play		Willie Park Jnr	155	Laidlay	162
1890	Prestwick	164	lst	John Ball	164	Ball	164
1891	St Andrews	177	12th=	Hugh Kirkaldy	166	Fergusson	170
1892	Muirfield	308	2nd=	Harold Hilton	305	Hilton	305
1893	Prestwick	332	8th=	W. Auchterlonie	322	Laidlay	324
1894	Sandwich	341	13th=	J.H. Taylor	326	Tait	340
1895	St Andrews	344	18th=	J.H. Taylor	322	Tait	341
1896	Muirfield	Did not play		Harry Vardon	316	Tait	319
1897	Hoylake	334	17th	Harold Hilton	314	Hilton	314
1898	Prestwick	Did not play		Harry Vardon	307	Hilton	309
1899	Sandwich	339	25th=	Harry Vardon	310	Tait	324
1900	St Andrews	Did not play		J.H. Taylor	309	Maxwell	329
1901	Muirfield	Did not play		James Braid	309	Hilton	320
1902	Hoylake	323	15th=	Sandy Herd	307	Maxwell	309
1903	Prestwick	Did not play		Harry Vardon	300	Maxwell	318
1904	Sandwich	318	18th	Jack White	296	Graham	310
1905	St Andrews	Did not play		James Braid	318	—	
1906	Muirfield	321	35th=	James Braid	300	Graham	306
1907	Hoylake	327	15th=	Arnaud Massy	312	Graham	326
1908	Prestwick	311	13th=	James Braid	291	Ball	311
1909	Deal	Did not play		J.H. Taylor	295	Lassen	308
1910	St Andrews	314	19th=	James Braid	299	Ball	314
1911	Sandwich	Failed to qualify		Harry Vardon	303	Hilton	304
1912	Muirfield	Failed to qualify		Ted Ray	295	Scott	327
1913	Hoylake	Did not play		J.H. Taylor	304	Graham	318
1914	Prestwick	Did not play		Harry Vardon	306	Jenkins	315

Note: He also entered for the 1924 Open at Hoylake but failed to qualify.

II Ball's Amateur Championship Record

Year	*Venue*	*Matches won*	*Round*	*Winner*	*John Ball lost to:*
1885	Hoylake	4	Semi-final	Macfie	Hutchinson
1886	St Andrews	4	Semi-final	Hutchinson	Lamb
1887	Hoylake	4	Final	Hutchinson	Hutchinson
1888	Prestwick	5	Winner	Ball	
1889	St Andrews	3	Semi-final	Laidlay	Laidlay
1890	Hoylake	5	Winner	Ball	
1891	St Andrews	1	2nd round	Laidlay	Sharp
1892	Sandwich	6	Winner	Ball	
1893	Prestwick	2	3rd round	Anderson	Fergusson
1894	Hoylake	6	Winner	Ball	
1895	St Andrews	5	Final	Balfour-Melville	Balfour-Melville
1896	Sandwich	3	4th round	Tait	Tait
1897	Muirfield	0	2nd round	Allan	Maxwell
1898	Hoylake	3	5th round	Tait	Robb
1899	Prestwick	7	Winner	Ball	
1900-1	Did not play				
1902	Hoylake	1	2nd round	Hutchings	Maxwell
1903	Muirfield	4	6th round	Maxwell	Macdonald
1904	Sandwich	3	4th round	Travis	Hutchinson
1905	Prestwick	0	1st round	Barry	Laidlay
1906	Hoylake	1	3rd round	Robb	Laidlay
1907	St Andrews	8	Winner	Ball	
1908	Sandwich	1	2nd round	Lassen	Pollock
1909	Muirfield	0	2nd round	Maxwell	Grant
1910	Hoylake	8	Winner	Ball	
1911	Prestwick	2	4th round	Hilton	Crummack
1912	Westward Ho!	7	Winner	Ball	
1913	St Andrews	0	1st round	Hilton	Pegler
1914	Sandwich	2	3rd round	Jenkins	Hambro
1915-20	No Championship or did not play				
1921	Hoylake	4	5th round	Hunter	Wright
1922-26	Did not play				
1927	Hoylake	0	2nd round	Tweddell	Abercrombie
		99			

III Club Scratch Medals

	Royal Liverpool	*Other*			*Medals Won*
1881	Dowie (84); Kennard (87); Milligan (86)				3
1882	Club Gold (83); Connaught (83); Dowie (80); Kennard (82)				4
1883	Club Gold (86); Lubbock (87); Kennard (82); Milligan (82)				4
1884	Connaught (83); Lubbock (82); Dowie (88)				3
1885	Club Gold (77); Lubbock (84); Dowie (87); Kennard (86)				4
1886	Lubbock (83); Dowie (83); Kennard (82) Milligan (85)				4
1887	Club Gold (79); Connaught (79); Lubbock (79); Dowie (84); Kennard (83); Milligan (80)				6
1888	Connaught (87); Lubbock (87); Dowie (81); Kennard (86); Milligan (83)	*St George's*	Grand Challenge Cup	(180)	6
1889	Club Gold (79); Connaught (83); Dowie (83)	*St George's*	Grand Challenge Cup	(169)	4
1890	Lubbock (82). Dowie (82); Milligan (87)	*St George's*	Grand Challenge Cup	(175)	4
1891	Club Gold (82); Dowie (82); Milligan (90)	*St George's*	Grand Challenge Cup	(174)	4
1892	Club Gold (86); Connaught (86); Dowie (82); Kennard (82); Milligan (78)				5
1893	Lubbock (84); Milligan (83)	*Chester*	Scratch Cup	(75)	4
		Lytham	Manchester	(82)	
1894	Milligan (82)	*St David's*	Scratch Bowl	(152)	5
		Lytham	Clifton	(82)	
			Manchester	(82)	
			Thistleton	(76)	
1895					
1896	Club Gold (83); Connaught (81); Kennard (76)				3
1897	Connaught (77); Milligan (79)	*Lytham*	Manchester	(78)	4
			Ladies	(80)	
1898	Lubbock (76); Dowie (76); Milligan (79)				3
1899	Dowie (77)	*Lytham*	Silver Iron	(160)	4
			Ladies	(75)	
			Thistleton	(74)	
1900					
1901		*Lytham*	Thistleton	(75)	1
1902		*Lytham*	Silver Iron	(157)	
			Clifton	(73)	
			Thistleton	(74)	3
1903	Club Gold (77); Connaught (75) Lubbock (81); Milligan (75)	*Lytham*	Silver Iron	(154)	
			Manchester	(75)	6

1904	Dowie (79); Kennard (78);	*Leasowe*	John Ball Shield	(74)	8
	Milligan (79)	*Lytham*	Silver Iron	(158)	
			Clifton	(72)	
			Manchester	(76)	
			Thistleton	(77)	
1905	Connaught (77); Milligan (79)	*Lytham*	Clifton	(75)	6
			Manchester	(75)	
			Ladies	(76)	
			Thistleton	(78)	
1906	Club Gold (80); Lubbock (76);	*Leasowe*	John Ball Shield	(77)	8
	Dowie (74); Kennard (73);	*Lytham*	Clifton	(80)	
	Milligan (84)		Ladies	(78)	
1907	Lubbock (80); Kennard (76);	*Leasowe*	John Ball Shield	(85)	5
	Milligan (82);	*Lytham*	Ladies	(73)	
1908	Club Gold (79); Connaught (80);	*Wallasey*	Harrison Medal	(76)	8
	Dowie (77); Kennard (75);	*Blackpool*	Open	(148)	
	Milligan (80)	*Leasowe*	John Ball Shield	(76)	
1909	Connaught (80)	*Wallasey*	Cullen Medal	(79)	4
		Formby	Prestwich	(78)	
			Fowler	(77)	
1910	Connaught (81); Lubbock (77)	*Leasowe*	Scinde Putter	(74)	3
1911	Connaught (78); Kennard (77)	*Lytham*	Clifton	(73)	6
			Ladies	(74)	
		Formby	Fowler	(76)	
			St Andrews	(78)	
1912	Connaught (75) Dowie (77)	*Leasowe*	Scinde Putter	(73)	3
1913	Kennard (76) Milligan (78)	*Leasowe*	Scinde Putter	(71)	4
			Doleman	(78)	
1914		*Leasowe*	John Ball Shield	(71)	1
1915/18	No competitions				
1919					
1920	Kennard (79)				1
1921	Club Gold (77)				1
1922	Club Gold (77)	*Leasowe*	John Ball Shield	(78)	3
			Doleman	(80)	
1923	Lubbock (76)				1
1924		*Leasowe*	Scinde Putter	(75)	1
1926		*Leasowe*	Doleman	(78)	1
1927		*Leasowe*	John Ball Shield	(77)	1
					149

Note: At Royal Liverpool gold medals were awarded as follows:

Club Gold Medal	:	1st day Spring Meeting
Duke of Connaught's Star	:	2nd day Spring Meeting
Lubbock Gold Medal	:	Summer Meeting
Dowie Cup	:	1st day Autumn Meeting
Kennard Gold Medal	:	2nd day Autumn Meeting
Milligan Gold Cross	:	St Andrews Meeting

In addition silver medals were awarded to runners-up in the Spring and Autumn Meetings. Ball won 19 of these silver medals, which are not included in this table.

IV Prestwick Links in 1890

(Extract from the *Saturday Review* of 31 May 1890 in the series 'Links not Missing' No. 3 Prestwick)

St Andrew's may be more royal and of older standing, but one probably may say of Prestwick, without fear of contradiction, that of all the golf links in the kingdom it is the most picturesque ... The eye of the harassed golfer may calm itself with contemplation of a wonderful panorama. On the south west the Heads of Ayr, guarding the entrance to the town—further out, like a lonely sentinel, Ailsa Craig, the home of the gannet; due west, bathed in a purple mist, where 'Arran's peaks are grey', Goat Fell and Holy Island; and a little to the northward the Cumbraes and all the glories of the Kyles of Bute.

But all the scenery, in the opinion of the golfer, is very pretty fooling, but has nothing whatever to do with golf, and he has nothing whatever to do with it. It does not affect him, and except when he is very many holes up, or very many holes down, so that a match has lost all its interest, and he has ceased to be a golfer, and become only an ordinary human being, he does not even look at it. But there is beauty in the striking features and up and down variety at the Prestwick links which forces itself upon him despite himself; for it affects him not as a human being, but in his real self, as a golfer. The course is so hilly, so faced with bold precipitous bunker cliffs, all the hazards are on so grand a scale, the sandhills are so mountainous, the burn is really worthy of its name! How many a golfer has been sadly disillusioned on his first sight of that famous Swilkan Burn of St Andrews, of which he had heard so much! A burn! it has such a find moorland sound. You can almost hear it rushing down between its alders, over its boulders. And what has he found? A muddy little dribble worming along ignominiously at a crawl, between little stone built walls, as if it would never get to the sea. An eel would scorn to live in it. But the Prestwick burn has a semblance of the real article. There are no alders, but it bustles along at a good merry pace between green banks, and is a wholesome looking little stream, which will carry your ball far away down before you can overtake it, if ever you do. A trout might live in it. It is said that many do, and that their flesh is of a peculiarly elastic firmness and piquant flavour, which analysis shows to be due to the presence of gutta-percha in large quantities.

Prestwick itself is a nice little collection of villas. It has a beach and sands ... The Prestwick Clubhouse is a more solid, habitable looking mansion than the Westward Ho! conventicle, though it does not rival the stately majesty of the St Andrew's Club. Prestwick is a few minutes run by rail from Ayr, and from the Prestwick station to the Clubhouse goes a private passage sacred to members only. The profane vulgar are kept at a discreet distance. Prestwick has many merits, but this is not its least — that its links are the private property of the Club ...

Prestwick golfers of today ... tee their balls just in front of the Clubhouse, with a high wall, bounding the railway, on the right of the course to the first hole. A straight drive meets no hazard, and from a good lie you may loft over bunkery ground onto the putting green. A heeled ball means perdition and the railway; but your caddie can retrieve your ball, unless it has gone into the window of a passing train, in which case you telegraph for it to the Station Master at Troon ... The second hole is an iron shot. You may do it in one, but may think yourself lucky if you do it in three. A fine drive to the third brings you to the brink of the deep deep bunker named with fitting reverence the 'Cardinal's Nob'. It is wide as well as deep. On its right rushes the burn, wherein dwell the trout who batten on golf balls. The Nob rises precipitous on the far side of the bunker, a great cliff of sand, shored up with timbers of black forbidding aspect. To be digging with niblick in this west coast Cardinal's sacred Nob is as sad a plight as befell the luckless jackdaw beneath the ban of His Eminence of Rheims. It was in this famous bunker that a new system of counting was inaugurated. 'How many have you played?' asked a golfer, who had patiently waited while his opponent played racquets against the black timbers. 'I don't know' said the sufferer wearily. 'I went in to the Nob at half past eleven; I've been playing ever since, and it's ten minutes to twelve now; you can calculate that for yourself.' It is the first authentic application of the time test to golf. If you fly the Nob with a good second, you will be within ironing range of the hole for your third.

For the fourth hole you tee on the nearside of a wall, and presuming you do not top into the wall, may go sailing along for two full shots over flat country, with the burn meandering on your right, and pernicious, benty ground to the left. The hole is cunningly ensconced in a bay of the Serpentine burn. You make a solemn vow to yourself that you will play well to the left; but the moment you have struck the ball the burn seems to meander further out into the course, and receiving your ball into its bosom, to return forthwith to its channels. It seems to do all this, but probably it is only seemingly, and, at all events you make up your mind that you will give it a good wide berth next time. And now you have come to the foot of the Himalayas — those mighty mountains. The Prestwick golfer will rue it, with much expense of lead pencil and scoring card, if he do not follow the imperial Roman's example in his drive over the Himalayas. For the tee is at the burn's edge and the sandhills rise very high before you. You may hit a fair shot and yet if it be not lofted high into the air, may find yourself in ravines of the higher Himalayas, above the line of perpetual bunker. Then, though the hole be short — a really fine cleek shot will reach it — the score is likely to be long. The Trans-Himalayan country is not of the same catastrophic nature as that we have left behind. No efforts of genius are needed for the next five holes—only straight and sober driving. The putting green of the hole next after the Himalayas is on a slope which makes it full of that uncertainty which the golfer loves. At the eighth hole the railway again presents itself within the range of practical politics; but the ball must needs be very badly heeled. Putting out for the tenth brings us again to the foot of the Himalayas. This time the drive is of more fearful import even than before; for do we not know, do we not see in our mind's eye, that rushing burn on the far side of the mountains? The caddies are on before us, on the mountain top. As the ball flies over the bunker there is a moment of fearful suspense; then a glad shout of 'Over!' cheers us, or the fatal verdict of 'In' dashes our hopes, and we say forbidden words. And so back again, between the bents and the burn, to a hole just over the little wall before which we teed when coming out. Then comes a long sandy hole near the bents by the seashore, and then, turning straight clubwards for the fourteenth hole, we putt out close under the windows of the Prestwick houses. We have gone the circuit and returned; but the autocrat St Andrew decrees eighteen holes as the number for a golf course; and out we go again on a sort of inner circle for four holes more. The fifteenth and sixteenth are over hazardous, broken ground, and the tee for the seventeenth is on the crest of an old friend, the Cardinal's Nob. It must be a very bad top for him to punish us this time, and we may hope to put ourselves within reach of the great deep valley in which the hole is ensconced. The hole is at the bottom; the valley's sides are of most beautiful velvety turf; there is delicious excitement in hurrying up the steep side facing us, to peep over and see how near the hole our well lofted shot has rolled. There is uncertainty—perhaps too much uncertainty—but the delights of the expectation and realisation stay with one long after all memory of the flat holes has vanished. Then from a tee set up on high we drive to within an iron shot of the last hole, and soon the weary golfer is at rest.

Prestwick used to be a twelve hole course. All those holes beyond the wall, including of course the great Himalayas, are a modern extension. And the seventeenth hole, deep down in its valley, may be taken as a type of the holes of the old Prestwick course. Prestwick has lost something by its conformity to the orthodox eighteen, but has probably gained far more.

V Songs and Verse

'John Ball' — sung to the tune of 'Do you ken John Peel'
(St Andrews Dinner 1890)

Solo Do you ken John Ball who at golf doth play,
Who went to Scotland the other day,
And brought the great Championship away
To his home by the Dee in the morning.

Refrain Yes, we ken John Ball and Charlie too,
'Brassy' and 'Bulger' and 'Driver' so true,
And we ken his grand score of twice eight-two,
On Prestwick links in the morning.

Solo Do you ken John Ball, when he leads the way
Round the 'course' in golfing array?
And his halloo of 'fore' strike his foes with dismay,
When it's heard on the links in the morning.

Refrain Yes we ken John Ball and his 'fore' halloo
His 'Cleek' and his 'Iron' and his 'Niblick' too,
His stroke from the 'tee' sends his ball out of view,
When he's out on the links in the morning.

Solo Do you ken John Ball, and his modest way—
Of his skills supreme makes no display;
But is ready to meet the best in the fray
In 'foursome' or 'single' in the morning.

Refrain Yes we ken John Ball and his modesty too,
His skillful play, and his heart so true
And his Champion score of twice eighty-two
On Prestwick links in the morning.

'The Championship'—(*Daily Post* 29 May 1899)

Our Johnny's champion once again,
Good old Johnny Ball,
And what a triumph o'er the Thane,
Good old Johnny Ball,
When plucky Saxon, gallant Celt,
Stepped out to battle for the belt,
What lungeous drives were featly dealt,
Good old Johnny Ball.

How swayed the battle to and fro,
Good old Johnny Ball,
The Gael above, the Saxon low,
Good old Johnny Ball,
How when the fight seemed all but lost,
The bunker and the burn he crossed,
The long approach he deftly tossed,
Good old Johnny Ball.

Quick pulsed each Saxon heart that beat,
For good old Johnny Ball,
And paled each cheek that feared defeat
For good old Johnny Ball,
But see! He wears his rival down,
He snatches victory and the crown,
Was ever gained such pluck's renown!
Good old Johnny Ball.

Yet what of him who led the Scotch,
Good old Freddy Tait,
That handsome soldier of the Watch
Good old Freddy Tait,
Yon splendid man of nerve and thew,
Who fought the glorious battle through,
Well, here's a Saxon cheer for you,
Good old Freddy Tait.

So may we struggle many a day,
The Saxon and the Gael,
And lose or triumph as we may,
The Saxon and the Gael,
Join friendly heart and honest hand,
That jar not, nor misunderstand,
And boast one common Fatherland,
The Saxon and the Gael.

'John's the Boy' — sung to the tune of 'Jack's the Boy'
(St Andrews Dinner 1899)

Of all the lads that be,
There is only one for me,
And his home by the Mersey's fragrant shore;
His demeanour it is shy
To the stranger who is nigh,
But his name will be remembered ever more
And his deeds will be forgotten,
When our men of war are rotten,
And 'tis then indeed will come the end of all;
'Well! who is the man?' 'tis cried,
And we answer in our pride
'Tis Johnny, yes, it's young John Ball'.

Chorus:

John's the boy for me
John's the boy for thee,
John's the lad, when England's sad
To challenge F.G.T. Ah!
Hard as nails his nerve
Grim as death, his mien:
John, our guest! you're quite the best
The world has ever seen

Hear the ringing of his cleek,
See his brassy delving deep,
Watch his matchless drives a'soaring in a gale;
And the wretch can putt all right,
When there's honour in the fight,
And never from a bunker doth he fail.
When some said his day was o'er
Straightway rose he keen once more,
And at Prestwick showed himself the best of all;
Yet again, when someone says
'To whom this mead of praise?'
With a will, reply we 'Young John Ball'

Chorus:

'John's the boy for me', etc.

No braggart is J.B,
But as modest as can be,
Of his deeds you never hear for aught he says;
But when Johnny buckles to
You may learn a thing or two,
And sell your shirt to back him, for it pays;

For upon the final pinch
He is never seen to flinch
Full of jannock bulldog British pluck is he;
So we'll spend no time in wondering
At his feats, but join in thundering
The best of luck to dear J.B.

Chorus: 'John's the boy for me', etc.

'Home' — poem by 'West Kirbyite' to honour the return of John Ball from the Boer War

The call 'to arms!' resounded over land and over sea,
When gallant little Hoylake, in responding to the call,
Sent out a representative, to show the enemy,
How England answered 'Ready' even to a human 'Ball'!

The son of England's glory, in the peaceful days of yore,
Fought cannily for Hoylake where the golf balls flew about
Until with mightier purpose, he essayed a nobler score,
Where the hail of British bullets stormed the enemy's redoubt.

Three cheers! and yet three more! to bid our hero welcome home!
'God bless our gallant khaki boys — we need them, one and all!
Be this our toast, — and further, let each heart within us own
That we answered Kruger rarely when we sent a Hoylake 'Ball'

'Johnnie Ball' by Mr Ronald Ross

When Balfour's magnetism bright,
And his electric flame
O'er Britain's kingdom flashed the light
Of the old historic game,
'Twas then a young disciple sprung,
Obedient to his call,
To show the way how golf to play,
His name was Johnnie Ball.

What need to tell what Johnnie's done,
Or of each golfing feat,
Of records made, and matches won,
They're known where golfers meet;
On every green where he has been
Its habitués recall,
With keen delight, the golfing might
And strength of Johnnie Ball.

Go, watch him, posing at the place
Where his ball sits on the tee,
His polished style, its ease and grace,
And his swing so strong and free;
His quarter strokes your praise provokes,
And, at the putting role,
His ball runs true, as if it knew,
The road to every hole.

Whene'er, by luck's erratic vein,
He from his game falls off,
'Tis to come out on top again
With a burst of splendid golf.
With science, skill, instinct, and will,
All ready at his call;
His genius fired, his soul inspired,
That's brilliant Johnnie Ball.

Thou darling golf, my mistress dear,
For thee alone I live;
I would not miss thy smiles sincere,
For all that earth can give;
Thy constant charm each feeling warms,
And holds each thought in thrall,
When I, the sage with thee engage,
Or watch young Johnnie Ball.

Our gallant yeomen, all who live
Their merits must confess,
Whether on fields of sport they strive,
Or in war's bitter stress;
When late, the state, in danger great,
Upon its sons did call,
The first to go to meet the foe,
Was plucky Johnnie Ball.

England, the first in every game,
In which it takes a pride,
In golf, a game it once thought tame,
Has ta'en a wondrous stride;
It now can boast a growing host,
Of golfers great and small,
But few among its golfing throng
Can match young Johnnie Ball.

Long may he play the honest game
He's played so long and well,
To add fresh lustre to his fame,
And newer records tell;
And when death dour, with putts dead sure,
Has holed us golfers all,
When you and I forgotten lie,
They'll talk of Johnnie Ball.